Physical Characteri Chow Cho

(from The Kennel Club b

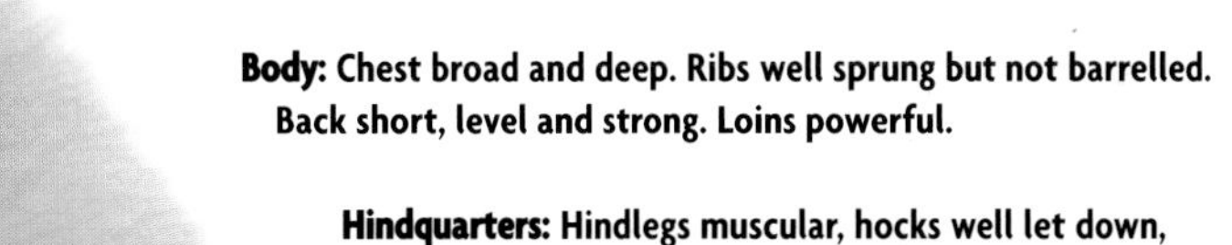

Body: Chest broad and deep. Ribs well sprung but not barrelled. Back short, level and strong. Loins powerful.

Hindquarters: Hindlegs muscular, hocks well let down, with minimal angulation, essential to produce characteristic stilted gait. From hocks downwards to appear straight, hocks never flexing forward.

Feet: Small, round, cat-like, standing well on toes.

Tail: Set high, carried well over back.

Coat: Either rough or smooth.
Rough: Profuse, abundant, dense, straight and stand-off. Outer coat rather coarse in texture, with soft woolly undercoat. Especially thick round neck forming mane or ruff and with good culottes or breechings on back of thighs.
Smooth: Coat short, abundant, dense, straight, upstanding, not flat, plush-like in texture.
Any artificial shortening of the coat which alters the natural outline or expression should be penalised.

Colour: Whole coloured black, red, blue, fawn, cream or white, frequently shaded but not in patches or parti-coloured (underpart of tail and back of thighs frequently of a lighter colour).

Size: Dogs: 48–56 cms (19–22 ins) at shoulder. Bitches: 46–51 cms (18–20 ins) at shoulder.

Chow Chow

by Eric Freeman

Table of Contents

PUBLISHED IN THE UNITED KINGDOM BY:

INTERPET PUBLISHING

Vincent Lane, Dorking
Surrey RH4 3YX
England

ISBN 1-902389-49-2

The publisher would like to thank Barbara Bakert, Ernie Coy, Pat Rose, Karen Tracy and the rest of the owners of dogs featured in this book.

Photos by Carol Ann Johnson, with additional photos by:

BJ Andrews
Norvia Behling
TJ Calhoun
Carolina Biological Supply
Doskocil
Isabelle Francais
James Hayden-Yoav
James R Hayden, RBP
Bill Jonas
Alice van Kempen
Dwight R Kuhn
Dr Dennis Kunkel
Mikki Pet Products
Antonio Philippe
Phototake
Jean Claude Revy
Alice Roche
Dr Andrew Spielman
C James Webb

Illustrations by Renée Low

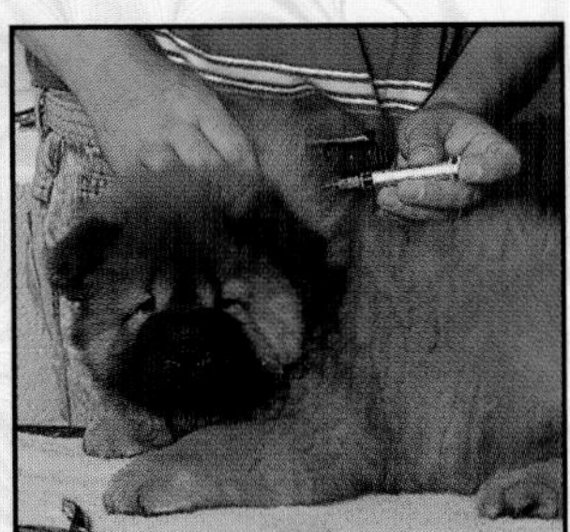

One of China's legendary dogs, the Chow Chow has been used for hunting, caravan guarding, sampan and junk guarding and for food. It is also a superior pet for the right owner, though it has never achieved pet status in China.

HISTORY OF THE CHOW CHOW

The romantic tales surrounding the origin of the beautiful and temperamentally unique Chow Chow are countless. The somewhat blurred origins and unusual looks of this breed have led to legendary and fanciful links to all kinds of animals outside the canine world. Not the least of these legends is the one that claims it is the bear rather than the wolf from which the Chow descends.

There is nothing to substantiate the Chow's relationship to the bear, but those who choose to believe this cite many characteristics that the breed shares with no other animal but the bear. Supporters of this theory claim that a form of primitive wild animal, which is now extinct, is the ancestor of the Chow.

All other dogs are known to have descended from the progenitors of the wolf. This, according to the bear theorists, explains why most other dogs either look away from the Chow Chow at first meeting or immediately prepare themselves to attack.

When one stops to consider the bear's independent nature, its blue tongue and the stilted manner in which it walks—all characteristics of the Chow Chow—it becomes understandable how the theory took root. There is also the remarkable resemblance of the bear cub to the Chow. If nothing else, all this makes one wonder if Mother Nature just might have lent some ironic twist to the evolution of the Chow.

Although China embraces the Chow Chow as one of its own, historical documents originating in China consistently refer to the breed as 'the foreign Chow.' This substantiates the more scientific research that reveals the Chow was of Arctic origin migrating to China with the barbarian tribes that frequently invaded China in the 11th century BC.

These barbarian invaders had dogs of formidable size that were described as having black tongues and being so fierce that they could easily bring down humans as if they were straws. These warrior dogs sometimes resembled

DID YOU KNOW?

Dogs and wolves are members of the genus *Canis*. Wolves are known scientifically as *Canis lupus* while dogs are known as *Canis domesticus*. Dogs and wolves are known to interbreed. The term *canine* derives from the Latin derived word *Canis*. The term *dog* has no scientific basis but has been used for thousands of years. The origin of the word dog has never been authoritatively ascertained.

lions in colour as well as in their head characteristics. They also had long claws and shaggy manes that covered their necks.

Though the Chow's long existence in China can be traced through its image on bronzes and in paintings, much of the breed's documented history was destroyed by the Emperor Chin Shih who wantonly destroyed most of China's literature in 225 BC. The records that did survive add some interesting details to the earlier descriptions of the warrior dogs.

These writings describe the dogs as being completely different from other breeds of dog with large broad heads, short muzzles and small eyes. The lips are described as not overlapping but just touching, giving them a unique aloof expression.

It appears that although these warrior dogs were devoted to their keepers, they were extremely hostile to strangers. Their fierce natures made them ideal candidates for their roles as war dogs. It is interesting to note that these same dogs proved to be excellent hunters and herding dogs.

As centuries passed, the breed's fierce nature mellowed and the dogs could be assigned duties of a more domestic nature: draught dog, hunter, herder, guardian of the home and, unfortunately for the dogs, as food for the family as well.

The Chinese (and subsequent English) slang word

DID YOU KNOW?

Since dogs have been inbred for centuries, their physical and mental characteristics are constantly being changed to suit man's desires for hunting, retrieving, scenting, guarding and warming their masters' laps. During the past 150 years, dogs have been judged according to physical characteristics as well as functional abilities. Few breeds can boast a genuine balance between physique, working ability and temperament.

for something edible is 'chow.' The dogs kept for this purpose were considered a great delicacy. Thus, dog meat was sold and eaten throughout China and Korea until it was prohibited by law in China in 1915.

Chinese legend gives us purely practical reasons for two of the Chow's most distinguishing characteristics: the straighter the hind leg, the more abundant the meat; and the bluer the tongue, the more tender and delicious the meat.

WEST MEETS EAST

There can be no doubt that as the first clipper ships entered Chinese harbours, British sailors were fascinated by the multitude of curiosities this strange country afforded. Certainly not the least of these oddities was this dog that was more bear- or lion-like than anything ever seen by British seamen. It is little wonder the sailors took their canine curiosities back to England with them on return voyages. In 1780 the first Chows arrived in Great Britain.

At the turn of the 20th century, China was exporting short-coated Chows. They were called edible dogs and according to Customs forms they were considered food animals like swine, chickens and ducks.

Little is known of the fate of those first exotic immigrants to England. It was not until 1840 that a newspaper account tells of several Chows who were kept in the London Zoological Park. They were referred to as the 'wild dog of China.'

In 1880, however, records document the exhibition of Chinese Puzzle, a black Chow female imported directly from China. Chinese Puzzle was shown at a dog show that took place at the famous Crystal Palace in London. Evidently the look of Chinese Puzzle

The Chinese Foo Dog is suspected of being a direct relative of the Chow Chow.

The Chinese Foo Dog derives from the same stock as the ancient Chow Chow. Although considered a rare breed around the world today, this 'teddy bear' of a dog is among the most affectionate and intelligent of companion animals.

Barbara J Andrews, famous American dog breeder and author, campaigned some of the first Chinese Foo Dogs in the States, adding the Foo Dog to the other breeds for which Mrs Andrews is known, including the Japanese Akita, Miniature Bull Terrier, Rottweiler, and most recently the Chihuahua. The Foo Dog is traditionally clipped in the fashion of the lion and can be seen in a variety of colours.

caught the eye and captured the fancy of some of London's most fashionable ladies including the Marchioness of Huntley.

When the Marchioness was offered a Chow that her relative, the Earl of Lonsdale, had brought back from China, she not only accepted the gift but immediately requested the Earl bring back more of the dogs on his next trip. Upon the arrival of the new dogs, Lady Huntley set about breeding Chows, heading up the kennel with an imported male she named Periodot.

A Periodot daughter, Periodot II, bred by the Marchioness was subsequently sold to Lady Granville Gordon who established a highly respected breeding kennel on the blood of this female. Lady Gordon's daughter, Lady Faudel-Phillips, shared her interest in the Chow Chow and became the most important and influential breeder in England. The Ladies Gordon and Phillips were to produce the first English-bred champion Chow who was named simply Blue Blood.

Lady Faudel-Phillips, circa 1932, with one of her Amwell Chows. The Amwell kennels produced many champion Chows.

The Chow Chow Club was formed in 1895 and an official standard of the breed was drawn up at the first meeting. The club's first show for the breed was held at Westminster in the same year. It is interesting to note that the same standard, with only minor adjustments, continues to exist to this day and has been used as a basis for practically every other standard around the world.

By December of that same year, the Chow Chow Club was

DID YOU KNOW?

As early as the first century AD, Romans had classified dogs into six general groups: House Guardian Dogs, Shepherd Dogs, Sporting Dogs, War Dogs, Scent Dogs and Sight Dogs. Most dogs we know today can trace their ancestry directly back to dogs from these groups. Many other breeds were developed by combining two or more individuals from those original groups to create yet another 'breed.'

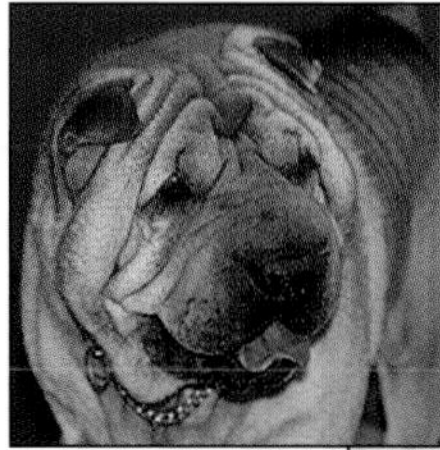

Shar Pei

DID YOU KNOW?

The Chow Chow shares his blue-black tongue with another Chinese pure-bred dog, the Shar Pei. This breed, only recently saved from the brink of extinction by dog fanciers around the world, continues to grow in popularity. Once called the Chinese Fighting Dog, the Shar Pei today is prized as a companion dog and show dog in many countries around the world.

able to stage its first show and no less than 54 Chows were entered. The impressive turnout of dogs was the talk of the dog fancy and helped the breed secure a position of respect amongst die-hard dog fanciers throughout the country.

When Lady Gordon died, her daughter Lady Phillips fell heir to all of the Chows. With these dogs and some of her own, Lady Phillips established the legendary Amwell Chow Chow Kennel in 1919. The kennel was to remain in operation until Lady Phillips' death in 1943.

With the breed in the hands of England's wealthy and titled men and women, the Chow Chow flourished. The breed's

The British dog breeder, Miss Joshua, was famed for the beautiful expressive faces of her dogs. The Chow look has been described as 'scowling' but many observers describe the breed as leonine, or lion-like.

Mrs Scaramanga's champion Chows were painted by Maud Earl in the 1930s.

DID YOU KNOW?

Ch Choonam Brilliantine was sold to America in 1925 for the then fantastic sum of £1800. At that time a modest house could have been purchased in England for half that amount.

fanciers could well afford huge kennels and the talented stockmen it took to manage them. The breed grew in number and in quality.

The first Chow Chow to become an English champion was an import, Ch Chow VIII, which was described as a dog of good type though somewhat lacking in coat. Unfortunately Chow VIII had a temperament that left much to be desired. Though his nasty temperament resulted in frequent changes of ownership, it barely affected Chow VIII's show career, which was somewhat spectacular for the day. Temperament notwithstanding, it is believed England's standard of the breed was written with Chow VIII as its model.

As years progressed, word of these mighty and exotic dogs spread to Europe and to America. In Europe it became a mark of distinction amongst the wealthy to own one of the edible wild dogs of China. While high prices were paid for the dogs in Europe, the breed was not really accepted by

DID YOU KNOW?

Ch Choonam Hung Kwong was the first of his breed to win Best in Show at Crufts Dog Show. He created a minor sensation, as he was described as 'a magnificent specimen...arrogant and proud, with great presence.'

In an illustration dated 1934, Vere Temple captured the antics of grandfather Chow looking over a litter only a few weeks old.

(Above) In 1933 this Chow, Ch Rochow Dragoon, held the record of winning 31 Challenge Certificates. He was famed for his cat-like feet and bold body, to say nothing of his other outstanding characteristics.

(Right) A head study of Ch Rochow Dragoon, the world's greatest Chow champion of the time. His head exhibits all of what is desired in the breed: the full ruff, the 'scowl' and the overall leonine look.

serious dog fanciers there until many years later.

In England the Chow Chow was forced to survive the devastating effects of two World Wars. With the determination so typical of the English, fanciers not only helped the breed inch forward through the worst of times but actually brought the breed to a resplendent level of quality shortly after World War II. There can be no doubt the breed owes its celebrated status throughout the world to England and the great dog men and women who embraced the 'edible wild dog of China' and shaped it into the loved and respected breed it is today.

One of Queen Alexandra of Britain's favourite breeds was the Chow Chow. Note the difference in type between Her Majesty's pet (seated in chair) and the Chows of today.

One of Lady Faudel-Phillips' delightful Chow puppies, a three-month-old who already bears the regal expression of an adult.

THE CHOW CHOW IN THE UNITED STATES

As the Chow increased in number and quality in Britain, the breed was attracting a mighty following in America as well. The first Chow to be exhibited in the United States appears in the 1890 catalogue of the Westminster Kennel Club, and 1905 is the most important date to be noted in the breed's American history according to famed breeder, judge and breed historian, Dr Samuel Draper.

In that year Mrs Charles E Proctor founded her Blue Dragon Kennels in America

This Egyptian pottery piece from thousands of years ago shows a resemblance to the Chow. A noted similarity is the carriage of the tail curved over the back.

and in that same year Mrs Proctor imported Chinese Chum, destined to become America's first champion Chow. Veterans of the breed consider Ch Chinese Chum to be the cornerstone of the breed in the United States.

It is to the credit of Chow Chow breeders and fanciers of the world throughout the 1950s and 1960s that great emphasis was placed upon the temperament and image of the breed. Great strides were made in these areas by one and all who bred dogs of superior type as well as calm and reliable temperament. Indeed, Dr Samuel Draper led the Chow temperament crusade, effectively changing the breed's reputation as a naturally unfriendly, even nasty dog. Dogs bred and campaigned by Dr Draper possessed ideal people-loving temperaments, as well as proper construction, gait and coat quality.

The Chow Chow of today has risen above its ill-gotten reputation of the past and stands proudly amongst man's most popular and devoted companions. For the person who takes the time to understand the character of the Chow Chow, there can be no greater canine friend.

DID YOU KNOW?

An ancient Chinese legend tells us that when the Chow Chow barked and the dark tongue was exposed, it was certain to ward off evil spirits. The dogs thus became highly regarded as guardians of Chinese temples.

Ch Rochow Diadem, owned by Mr Rotch, was the winner of 12 Challenge Certificates and is a wonderful example of the correct proportions, squareness and forward-tilting ear carriage of the modern Chow Chow.

This 1934 series of drawings and captions shows those faults of the Chow that were of most concern to dog judges.

Incorrect back leg.
Angular hock.
Tail set too low.

Too low on leg.
Down on pasterns.
Harefeet; pointed & narrow.

Tucked up.
(Upward slope of ventral line)
Tail falling to one side.

Narrow chest.

Pointed muzzle.

Eyes too round.
Large ears, too narrowly set.

'Chippendale' legs.

Out at shoulder.

Too high on leg.

Narrow chested.
(as made to stand in ring).

CHARACTERISTICS OF THE CHOW CHOW

Intrigued by the exotic history of the Chow Chow? Enchanted by the roly-poly bear cub appearance of a Chow puppy? You aren't alone! In fact, those two things alone have caused the Chow Chow to soar to heights of popularity on more than one occasion in the breed's history, but unfortunately it was to the detriment of the breed. Unscrupulous buyers rushed forth to capitalise on demand for the breed and bad temperaments were ignored.

A Chow Chow is an absolutely wonderful breed—for the right person! Before dashing out to buy a Chow—in fact before thinking about buying any dog—a person should definitely sit down and think the prospect out thoroughly. Teddy-bear-like Chow puppies snuggled together fast asleep one on top of the other are absolutely irresistible, I assure you. The Chow puppy's attractiveness as a subject for photography puts them on calendars and greetings cards around the world. This is a good part of what encourages well-meaning but misguided individuals to dash out to buy a Chow puppy for themselves or as a gift for someone they know that 'should have' a dog.

This is not to say the pudgy little ball of fluff you bring home will not be as cute and entertaining as those calendar pin-up pups. There is no doubt about that. However, calendars and greeting cards do not address the reality of dog ownership. Real Chow Chow puppies spend their days investigating, digging, chewing, eating, relieving themselves, having tummy aches and needing trips to the veterinary

DID YOU KNOW?

Chow Chows are perfectly content to live their lives out with the person or people in their own household and have no real need for attention from others. However, the Chow Chow that is not given proper socialisation can become introverted and sullen, often cross, with people whom they do not know.

NO SUCH THING AS . . .

There is no such thing as a 'bargain puppy.' Breeders charge realistic prices for their dogs

based upon the amount of time and effort (to say nothing of the money) they invest in producing sound, healthy stock with reliable temperaments. Deciding on a puppy because it is bargain priced may cost you a great deal of money at the veterinary clinic to compensate for the care that was not taken in the pup's parents.

surgeon for inoculations and so many other minor problems.

Puppies don't come pre-educated. Everything that you think a well-behaved dog should know how to do will have to be taught. Chows learn quickly but that is not to say they may feel it is entirely necessary to respond to your request. It takes time and patience to get through to a Chow, and the question you must ask yourself is whether or not you have the time and patience to do this educating.

WHO WINS THE PRIZE?

Who will ultimately be responsible for the dog's day-to-day care? Does that individual really want a dog? If you are the only person who needs to answer that question, there is no problem. However, all too often it is your spouse, your mother or father or anyone living in your home who will also share the responsibility of caring for the dog. The Chow Chow must be welcomed and wanted by all members of your household, or it will become a burden to all.

Mothers seem to fall into this role naturally—not necessarily because they want to, but the mothers I know are not inclined to stand by and watch any creature be neglected. Thus, it is 'mum' who takes the dog to the vet, who rushes out to buy the dog food and who takes the dog out for a walk. Mum just may not want any more duties than she already has!

Children will promise just about anything in order to get a puppy, but the question that has to be addressed seriously is what will happen after the novelty of owning a new dog has worn off. Again, who will ultimately be responsible for the dog's care?

Even if the entire family thinks a dog would be a great idea, does the lifestyle and schedule of the household lend itself to the demands of proper dog care? Someone must always be available to see to a dog's basic needs: feeding, exercise, coat care, access to the outdoors when required, and so on. If you or your family are gone from morning to night or if you travel frequently and are away from home for long periods of time, the dog still must be cared for. Will someone willingly be present to do so? Are you prepared to pay the costs of frequent boarding at a kennel while you are gone?

You must also stop to think about the suitability of the breed for the household, whether household means half a dozen children and adults or just you. Very young children can be rough and unintentionally hurt a puppy by dropping, pulling at or hitting it. It also takes a lot of talking to convince a toddler that a Chow's tail is not a handle to be pulled. No self-respecting Chow Chow is going to enjoy that nor should it be expected to. Chows are not blest with the tolerance of a Labrador Retriever, nor the pain-endurance of a Mastiff or Staffordshire.

The Chow is not the dog for every family. Chow owners must, above all, be patient in raising and training their dogs.

On the other hand, as a tiny puppy grows into a large and enthusiastic young adult seemingly overnight, it can overwhelm and sometimes injure an infant or small child in an exuberant moment.

IS A CHOW THE RIGHT DOG FOR YOU?

The entire history of the Chow has been one of close association with people, but the breed has never been one that has had a need to lavish attention on the humans around him. The Chow Chow is inclined to be a one-person, or at best a one-family, kind of a dog. Visitors are fine but not necessary to a Chow's existence. They are homebodies who live to be with their owner. Not particularly in their owners' laps, mind you, but nearby—where they can make sure you don't get into trouble.

What kind of person should own a Chow? One word will

What looks like a lion except that it has a dark tongue...and barks? The Chow Chow is known the world over for his lion-like appearance.

describe the person—patient. If the Chow owner is patient, he will be rewarded with a life companion whose devotion knows no end and whose sense of humour knows no bounds.

Lady Dunbar of Mochrum, one of England's pioneer breeders of the Chow, described the breed as follows: "...The Chow has many noble qualities, his heart cannot be taken by storm, but, once given, it is yours forever..." Though written a hundred years ago, this description of the Chow's character remains as apt today as then.

I have owned many breeds of dogs. None has been so

independent, so humorous, so disdainful of strangers or absolutely devoted as the Chow. If moulding a dog's spirit to conform to your picture of the ideal canine companion is an important factor in dog ownership, consider a breed other than the Chow. You can guide a Chow in the direction you want it to go but you can't push it there. Nor can you be heavy handed. As rough and tumble as the breed might be, as sturdy a constitution as the Chow might have and as high as its tolerance for discomfort might be, a Chow is completely incapable of withstanding being struck in anger. This devastates the Chow and, if subjected to treatment of this nature, it can turn even the most amiable youngster into a neurotic and unpredictable adult.

This is not to say the Chow owner needs to or should be passive in raising and training a Chow. On the contrary, a Chow must start understanding household rules from the first moment he comes into your home. What it will take to accomplish this is patience and a firm but gentle hand. This does not mean a stern reprimand or a resounding slap on the floor with a folded newspaper can never be administered. Somehow, even the youngest Chow understands the difference between being corrected and being abused.

Essentially a one-person (or one-family) dog, the Chow requires much human companionship and interaction with his owner.

If your idea of keeping a dog is having it live outdoors with minimal owner interaction, please do not consider a Chow. The Chow must have constant human companionship and social interaction not only with its owner but also with all kinds of people and other dogs. The Chow raised without this social-isation can easily become introverted and sullen. The young Chow can pass through

Ch Choonam Moonbeam and Ch Choonam Chang Li are fine examples of Mrs V A Manoch's Choonam Kennel, which was famous in the 1930s for its very high prices and very high-quality Chows.

IS A CHOW RIGHT FOR YOU?

If a dog that thrills to training or following routines is what you consider an ideal pet and companion perhaps looking to a breed other than the Chow Chow would be a good idea. Chows are notoriously independent and are more apt to respond when they take the notion rather than to follow a command. Chows don't refuse to obey but they will take their time in deciding just when the response should take place.

an adolescent stage when it decides his owner or family is all that is necessary for his well-being and can become very anti-social unless made to understand this is unacceptable.

It is then up to the caring owner to help guide the Chow through this difficult stage. Patience, persistence and support will help your Chow through this awkward time, but it does take time and a commitment to stay out there with the 'bashful' youngster.

The Chow character is both unique and contradictory. The breed seems almost to come pre-housebroken. It is a lesson the breed seems to want to learn and once learned only a major catastrophe can get the adult to transgress. On the other hand, the breed has a stubborn streak a mile long.

Anyone who has lived with a Chow knows how quickly the breed understands what you are trying to teach. The experienced owner also knows how long it can be before the Chow chooses to comply. Stubbornness extends itself to everything the Chow learns. Do everything you possibly can to avoid having your Chow develop bad habits because once something is learnt (good or bad), it takes practically an act of Parliament before you will be able to convince your Chow to forget that habit.

Most Chows look at strangers on an impartial basis. Fine if their master decides to have friends come to call, just as fine if not. As indifferent as the Chow can be to the comings and goings of visitors, there is no indifference when it comes to an intruder! What appears to be the laziest Chow known to the free world can suddenly become a hurricane of protectiveness when someone tries to enter its premises without an invitation!

Then, too, Chows seem to make 'blanket judgements.' If your Chow sees the little boy next door as a kind and gentle playmate, all little children will probably be high on your Chow's list of favourite people. On the other hand, if the uniformed delivery man threatens or strikes your Chow, pity any other uniformed man who enters your premises! Make sure your Chow's initial introduction to people is a positive experience. You will be hard pressed to change your Chow's mind once it is made up.

This applies to change in ownership as well. Some adult Chow Chows may rehome easily. Most do not. A good many breeds are just as happy living in one place as another, just so long as they are well fed and well treated. Not so with the Chow!

Does Chow ownership sound like a challenge? If so, you have definitely gotten my message. There is no doubt that a Chow will be able to test you in every way possible, but I am inclined to believe it is all done to determine whether or not you are worthy of being in the Chow's presence. If you do qualify, you will have a companion the likes of whom you will never forget.

Throughout history, Chows have been natural show dogs. They do not suffer from 'stage fright' and consistently perform well in the ring, as this group of confident Chows from a 1931 show illustrate.

A cream-coloured Smooth Chow.

The freshly bathed and groomed Chow in full coat certainly presents a beautiful picture, but a Chow enjoys digging holes and traipsing through mud puddles as much as any other dog. This requires bathing and grooming and yes, house cleaning, because Chows do moult—both coat types, Rough and Smooth.

With time, practice, and the right grooming tools, you can keep your Chow always looking as though it just stepped out of the grooming parlour. Do note, however, I did say, with time, practice, and the right grooming tools!

MALE OR FEMALE?

While some individuals may have their personal preferences for the sex of their dog, I can honestly say that both the male and the female Chows make wonderful companions. The decision will have more to do with the lifestyle and intentions of the owner than differences between the sexes. The male is larger, grander and sometimes a bit more aggressive. He's also much more heavily coated. The female is a bit smaller and usually carries less coat. Still, there are some very laid-back males and some bitches who are a bit more high-strung.

Spaying the female and neutering the male will not change the character of your pet but will avoid the problems you will have to contend with should you to choose not to do so. Neutering also precludes the possibility of your pet adding to the extreme pet overpopulation problem that concerns environmentalists worldwide.

A black Rough Chow.

COAT TYPES

An important consideration that must be addressed is whether at least one of the Chow's owners is willing to assume the responsibility of coat care. To divide this responsibility among unwilling members of the family is sheer folly. The task will not be done well or, if it is done at all, not done properly.

As much as we admire the properly groomed Rough Chow's crowning glory, one must be realistic and understand the coat looks that way only because it is given time and attention. Fortunately, Chow lovers who do not want the additional responsibility of the Rough's coat have the option of selecting a Smooth puppy or adult. In this case you have all the Chow benefits without the work that maintaining that beautiful coat entails.

HEALTH CONSIDERATIONS

In the wild any genetically transferred infirmity that would interfere with a newborn animal's survival would automatically be eliminated from the gene pool. Inability to nurse, to capture food as an adult and to escape from a predator are obviously impairments that would shorten an animal's life very quickly.

We who control the breeding of our domesticated dogs are intent upon saving all the puppies in a litter, but in preserving life we also perpet-

PUPPY SELECTION

In choosing a Chow Chow puppy, a happy, healthy and extroverted puppy is the bottom line. Never select the shy shrinking violet that cowers in a corner nor, on the other hand, the

standoffish pup that growls or challenges a stranger. Both of these extremes can lead to problems in adulthood with which the average pet owner is not prepared to cope.

The best exercise for a Chow Chow is that which lets him spend time with his owner.

uate health problems. Our humanitarian proclivities thus have drawbacks as well.

Like all other breeds of domesticated dogs, Chows have their share of hereditary problems. As careful as long-time Chow breeders might be in the stock they choose for their breeding programmes, hereditary problems still do crop up.

The following represent problems that exist in the breed. This does not mean that the puppy you buy or the line from which it comes will necessarily be afflicted with any of these genetic disorders, but they should be discussed with the breeder from whom you acquire your dog. The reputable Chow breeder is aware of the following problems and should be more than willing to discuss them with you.

HIP DYSPLASIA

Hip dysplasia (HD) is a condition which is considered to be polygenetic. This means it is created by the interaction of several genes, making it extremely hard to predict. Although it can be detected in the individual adult dog, it is only the law of averages that reduces the occurrence when breeding individual dogs x-rayed clear of the problem.

Hip Dysplasia (HD)

Commonly referred to as HD, this is an orthopaedic problem that affects many breeds of dogs and Chow Chows are no exception. It is a malformation of the hip joints. It usually occurs bilaterally, meaning in both hips. It can occur in varying degrees from the mildest form, which is undetectable other than by x-ray, on through to extremely serious and painful cases, which may require surgery.

A simple explanation of the disease is as follows: The normal hip can best be described as a ball and socket arrangement. The upper bone of the rear leg (femur) has a head that should fit neatly and firmly into the socket of the pelvis. A well-knit ball and socket allows the femur to rotate freely within the socket but is held firmly in place. When hip dysplasia exists, the socket is shallow allowing the femur head to slip and slide to a greater or lesser degree. The more shallow the

DO YOU KNOW ABOUT HIP DYSPLASIA?

Hip dysplasia is a fairly common condition found in purebred dogs. When a dog has hip dysplasia, its hind leg has an incorrectly formed hip joint. By constant use of the hip joint, it becomes more and more loose, wears abnormally and may become arthritic.

Hip dysplasia can only be confirmed with an x-ray, but certain symptoms may indicate a problem. Your dog may have a hip dysplasia problem if it walks in a peculiar manner, hops instead of smoothly runs, uses his hind legs in unison (to keep the pressure off the weak joint), has trouble getting up from a prone position or always sits with both legs together on one side of its body.

As the dog matures, it may adapt well to life with a bad hip, but in a few years the arthritis develops and many dogs with hip dysplasia become cripples.

Hip dysplasia is considered an inherited disease and only can be diagnosed definitively when the dog is two years old. Some experts claim that a special diet might help your puppy outgrow the bad hip, but the usual treatments are surgical. The removal of the pectineus muscle, the removal of the round part of the femur, reconstructing the pelvis and replacing the hip with an artificial one are all surgical interventions that are expensive, but they are usually very successful. Follow the advice of your veterinary surgeon.

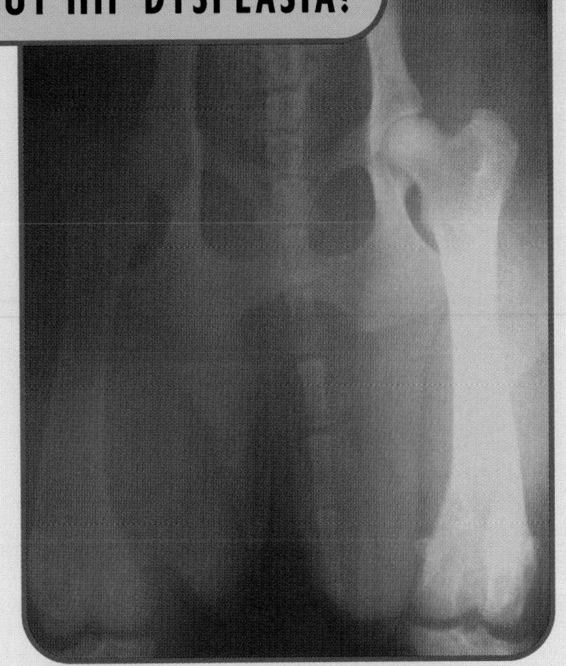

X-ray of a dog with 'Good' hips.

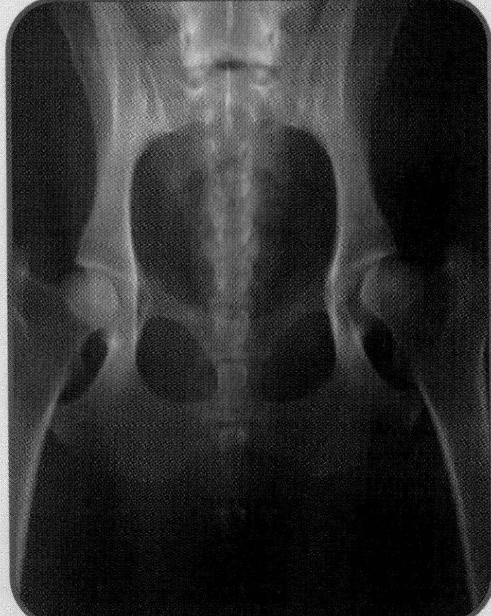

X-ray of a dog with 'Moderate' dysplastic hips.

A recent study found the Chow Chow with the biggest percentage of elbow dysplasia out of 170 breeds tested. Of the Chow Chows that were studied, almost 50 percent were dysplastic.

socket, the more it impairs movement and causes pain.

Osteochondritis Dissecans (OCD)

OCD is a condition in which the cartilage lining the bone surfaces in the shoulder joint, elbow or stifle and hock joints is thickened to the point where it enlarges and cracks, allowing the bone beneath it to become inflamed and deteriorate. The degree to which it takes place causes lameness varying from an occasional limp to a chronic condition. In Chows the area most commonly affected is the elbow and is referred to as elbow dysplasia (ED).

Eye Problems

Entropion: The eyelids are turned inward so that the eye lashes constantly rub against and irritate the eyeball itself. Untreated it can severely damage vision. A simple veterinary procedure can fully correct the condition.

Ectropion: A condition of the eyelid that causes the lid to roll out and hang down exposing the eye itself. The sagging eyelid forms a pocket that traps debris that constantly irritates the eye. This condition can also be corrected with surgery.

Patellar Luxation

The condition, also known as slipped stifle, can be found in one or both knees of the Chow. The ligament that holds the patella, or kneecap, in place can be so weak as to slip from the groove in which it would normally fit to bind the upper and lower thigh together. It can be painful and can cause limping in some cases.

The typical head of a quality Chow Chow, showing the characteristic purple tongue.

BREED STANDARD FOR THE CHOW CHOW

The Chow Chow with the right make and shape, balance and proportion is an imposing and beautiful sight to behold. The question arises, however, what is it that tells us if a Chow Chow does in fact have 'the right make and shape, balance and proportion'? Wouldn't the opinion of one fellow be as valid as the next?

Granted, your Chow Chow does not have to be a blue ribbon contender at Crufts Dog Show, but being 'blue-blooded' (pure-bred) does carry some responsibilities with it. There are characteristics for which the breed is noted and which your Chow Chow should possess.

A beautifully proportioned Chow Chow is an imposing sight. It is easy to see how some Chinese still refer to the Chow as the lion dog.

The answers to all that makes a Chow Chow an ideal specimen are found in The Kennel Club's breed standard. Breed standards are very accurate descriptions of the ideal specimen of a given breed. Standards describe the dog physically—listing all of a breed's anatomical parts and telling how those parts should look. The standard also describes the breed's temperament, how a dog should behave, and gait, how a well-made dog should move about.

This standard is the blueprint that breeders use to fashion their breeding programmes. The goal, of course, is to move one step closer to that ever elusive picture of perfection with each succeeding generation. The breed standard is also what dog show judges use to see which of the dogs being shown compares most favourably to what is required.

It should be understood that what the standard describes is the perfect dog of a given breed. In nature, nothing is absolutely perfect. Thus, the breeder and the judge are looking for the dog that in their opinion has 'most of the best.' How each individual person interprets this will always vary somewhat, but there is usually little disagreement when a dog comes along that truly has most of what the breed standard actually specifies. No dog will have it all.

Although it takes many years to fully understand the implications of a breed standard, it behoves the prospective owner of any breed to familiarise himself with the requirements therein. This will enable the person who wishes to own a dog of that breed to be able to have a good idea of what a representative specimen should look like.

THE KENNEL CLUB STANDARD FOR THE CHOW CHOW

General Appearance: Active, compact, short-coupled and essentially well balanced, leonine in appearance, proud, dignified bearing; well knit frame; tail carried well over back.

The general outline of a fully-coated Chow.

Characteristics: Quiet dog, good guard, bluish-black tongue; unique in its stilted gait.

Temperament: Independent, loyal, yet aloof.

Incorrect muzzle; too long and converging to a point.

A correctly shaped muzzle, broad and of moderate length.

Head and Skull: Skull flat, broad; stop not pronounced, well filled out under eyes. Muzzle moderate in length, broad from eyes to end (not pointed at end like a fox). Nose, large and wide in all cases, black (with exception of cream and near white in which case a light-coloured nose permissible, and in blues and fawns a self-coloured nose).

Eyes: Dark, oval shaped, medium sized and clean. A matching coloured eye permissible in blues and fawns. Clean eye, free from entropion, never being penalised for sake of mere size.

Ears: Small, thick, slightly rounded at tip, carried stiffly and wide apart but tilting well forward over eyes and slightly towards each other, giving peculiar characteristic scowling expression of the breed. Scowl never to be achieved by loose wrinkled skin of head.

Correct ears: carried forward over eyes and contributing to scowling expression.

Incorrect ear set and carriage.

Mouth: Teeth strong and level, jaws strong, with a perfect, regular and complete scissor bite, i.e. upper teeth closely overlapping lower teeth and set square to the jaws. Tongue bluish-black. Roof of mouth and flews black (blue black), gums preferably black.

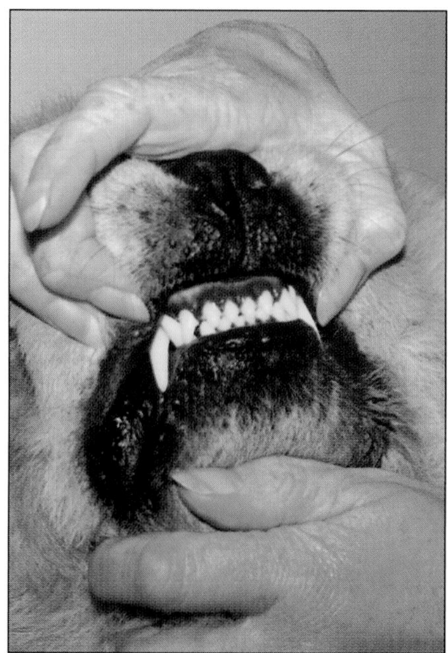

Correct Chow Chow bite.

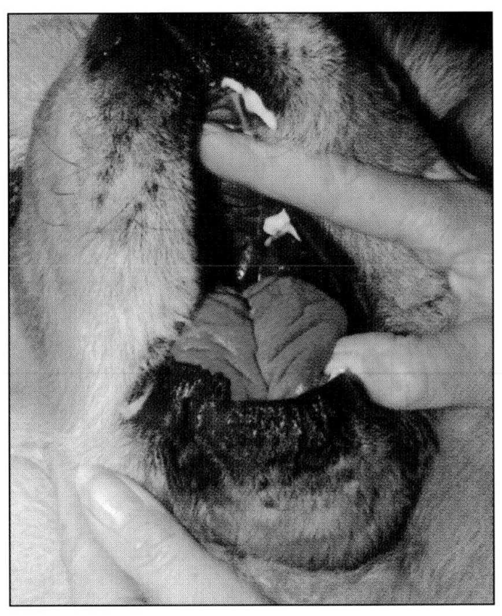

Characteristic purplish tongue; flews and roof of mouth are black.

Rear view of adult and pup showing correct tail set and carriage.

Neck: Strong, full, not short, set well on shoulders and slightly arched.

Forequarters: Shoulders muscular and sloping. Forelegs perfectly straight, of moderate length, with good bone.

Body: Chest broad and deep. Ribs well sprung but not barrelled . Back short, level and strong. Loins powerful.

Hindquarters: Hindlegs muscular, hocks well let down, with minimal angulation, essential to

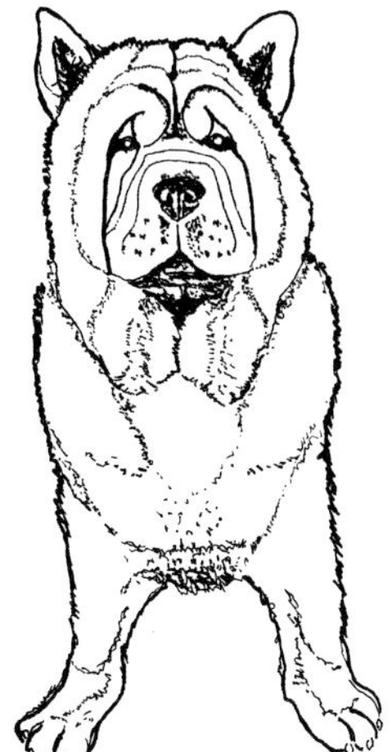

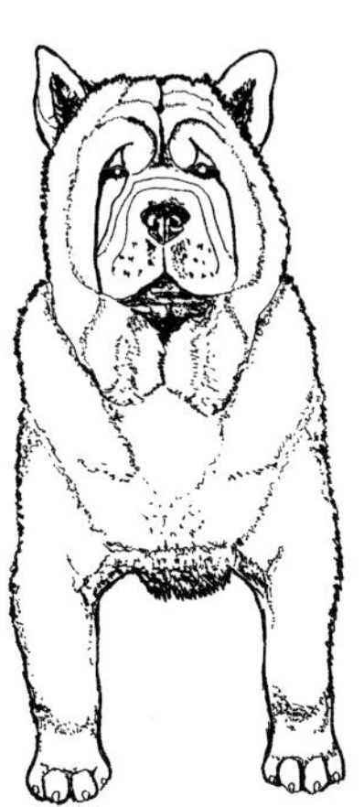

(left) Smooth Chow exhibiting weak forequarters, legs turned out. (middle) Rough Chow with legs that are too short. (right) Correct structure of forequarters, as shown in the Smooth Chow.

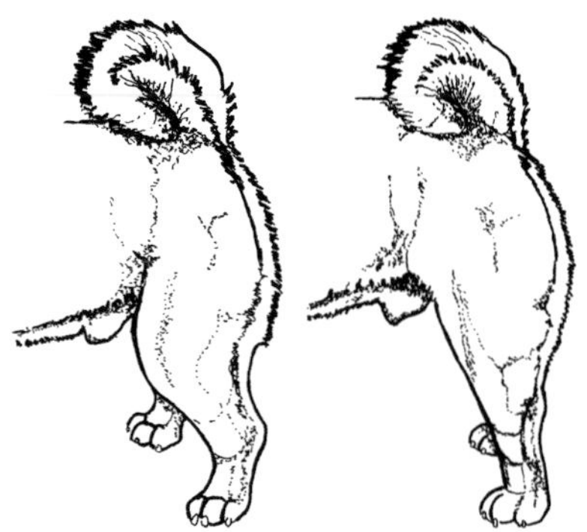

(Left) Weak hindquarters; over-angulated. (Right) Correct hindquarters with minimal angulation.

produce characteristic stilted gait. From hocks downwards to appear straight, hocks never flexing forward.

Feet: Small, round, cat-like, standing well on toes.

Tail: Set high, carried well over back.

Gait/Movement: Short and stilted. Forelegs and hindlegs moving parallel to each other and straight forward.

Coat: Either rough or smooth. *Rough:* Profuse, abundant, dense, straight and stand-off. Outer coat rather coarse in texture, with soft woolly undercoat. Especially thick round neck forming mane or ruff and with good culottes or breechings on back of thighs.

Smooth: Coat short, abundant, dense, straight, upstanding, not flat, plush-like in texture.

Any artificial shortening of the coat which alters the natural outline or expression should be penalised.

Colour: Whole coloured black, red, blue, fawn, cream or white, frequently shaded but not in patches or parti-coloured (underpart of tail and back of thighs frequently of a lighter colour).

The short, stilted gait of the Chow.

DID YOU KNOW?

According to The Kennel Club, 'The Breed Standard is the Blueprint of the ideal specimen in each breed approved by a governing body, e.g., The Kennel Club, the Fédération Cynologique International (FCI) and the American Kennel Club.

'The Kennel Club writes and revises Breed Standards taking account of the advice of Breed Councils/Clubs. Breed Standards are not changed lightly to avoid changing the standard to fit the current dogs and the health and well being of future dogs is always taken into account when new standards are prepared or existing ones altered.'

BREEDER'S BLUEPRINT

If you are considering breeding your bitch, it is very important that you are familiar with the breed standard. Reputable breeders breed with the intention of producing dogs that are as close as possible to the standard, and contribute to the advancement of the breed. Study the standard for both physical appearance and temperament, and make certain your bitch and your chosen stud dog measure up.

Size: Dogs: 48–56 cms (19–22 ins) at shoulder. Bitches: 46–51 cms (18–20 ins) at shoulder.

Faults: Any departure from the foregoing points should be considered a fault and the seriousness with which the fault should be regarded should be in exact proportion to its degree.

Note: Male animals should have two apparently normal testicles fully descended into the scrotum.

Ch Benchow the Tsaravich, Utility Group winner at a 1997 UK show. Owned by Mrs M E Bennett.

CHOW CHOW

WHERE TO BUY YOUR CHOW

Barring accidents, your Chow will live with you for many years. It is not at all surprising to see Chows live to be 10, 12 and often 14 years of age. It is extremely important, therefore, that the Chow puppy you purchase comes from a source where physical and mental soundness are primary considerations in the breeding programme.

Achieving this goal is usually the result of careful breeding over a period of many years. Selective breeding is aimed at maintaining the virtues of the breed and eliminating genetic weaknesses. Because this selective breeding is time-consuming and costly, good breeders protect their investment by providing the best prenatal care for their breeding females and nutrition for the growing puppies. There is no substitute for the amount of dedication and care good breeders give their dogs.

All this is not to imply your Chow puppy must come from a large kennel. On the contrary, many good puppies are produced by small hobby breeders in their homes. These names may well be included in recommendations from The Kennel Club and from local Chow Chow clubs. These individuals offer the same investment of time, study and knowledge as the larger kennel and often the puppies receive better hands-on socialisation, especially important with the Chow Chow breed.

Do not be surprised if a concerned breeder asks many questions about you and the environment in which your Chow will be raised. A responsible breeder will want to know if you have a fenced garden, if there are young children in the family and if someone will be home with the young puppy during the course of an average day. Good breeders are just as concerned with the quality of

DID YOU KNOW?

If the breeder from whom you are buying a puppy asks you a lot of personal questions, do not be insulted. Such a breeder wants to be sure that you will be a fit provider for his puppy.

DID YOU KNOW?

Your selection of a good puppy can be determined by your needs. A show potential or a good pet? It is your choice. Every puppy, however, should be of good temperament. Although show-quality puppies are bred and raised with emphasis on physical conformation, responsible breeders strive for equally good temperament. Do not buy from a breeder who concentrates solely on physical beauty at the expense of personality.

the homes to which their dogs are going as you, the buyer, are in obtaining a sound and healthy dog.

PURCHASING THE CHOW PUPPY

Most likely you are seeking a Chow for a companion dog and not necessarily for a show dog. If dog shows hold an interest, do let the breeder you are considering know this at the outset. Breeders are normally

Decide whether you want a pet-quality or show-quality Chow puppy before you start shopping.

INFORMATION...

Breeders rarely release puppies until they are eight to ten weeks of age. This is an acceptable age for most breeds of dog, excepting toy breeds, which are not released until around 12 weeks, given their petite

sizes. If a breeder has a puppy that is 12 weeks or more, it is likely well socialised and housetrained. Be sure that it is otherwise healthy before deciding to take it home.

most anxious to find show homes for those extra special puppies that come along every once in a while.

But if it is strictly a pet you are seeking, that does not mean you are looking for a second-rate model. A pet-quality Chow is not like a second-hand car or a 'slightly irregular' suit jacket. Your pet must be as sound, healthy and temperamentally fit as any top show dog.

Pet owners do not want a Chow who isn't sound of both body and mind, who is not trustworthy and reliable around children and strangers. Nor do they want one that doesn't look like a Chow. You are not buying a reject, you want an impressive dog with the leonine expression that typifies the breed—a dog that has sound hips, good eyes and a loveable personality.

Enquire about inoculations and when the puppy was last dosed for worms. Check the ears for any signs of mites or irritation. Are the eyes clear and free of any debris? The puppy coat is softer and fluffier than the adult coat and it should feel silky and clean to the touch. The Chow comes in an infinite variety of colours and if dog shows are not in your dog's future, the colour that appeals most to you is the one you should choose.

Never settle for anything less than a happy, healthy outgoing puppy. A Chow puppy should love the world and everyone in it. As playful as the puppy might be, it should not object to being held. Chow puppies that panic and struggle to be released have probably not had proper socialisation or might have inherited anti-social behaviour.

In total the Chow's head is massive and its expression is scowling and aloof. Perhaps less scowling and aloof in puppyhood but giving you an indication of what is to come.

Check the mouth to make sure that the bite is fairly even. Maturity can correct errors in dentition that are present at puppyhood, but never select a puppy that has any deformities of the mouth or jaw.

Pay attention to the way your selection moves. The Chow in puppyhood (particularly at eight weeks) is a miniaturised replica of what it looks like at maturity. Short and stylish looking with sound, deliberate movement, which may appear a bit wooden in puppyhood. There should be no inclination to stumble or limp. Do realise, though, that the chubby little boy puppies might be a bit more awkward than their slightly more svelte sisters, so do make allowances.

INFORMATION...

Your puppy should have a well-fed appearance but not a distended abdomen, which may indicate worms or incorrect feeding, or both. The body should be firm, with a solid feel. The skin of the abdomen should be pale pink and clean, without signs of scratching or rash. Check the hind legs to make certain that dewclaws were removed, if any were present at birth.

COMMITMENT OF OWNERSHIP

After considering all of these factors, you have most likely already made some very important decisions about selecting your puppy. You have chosen a Chow Chow, which means that you have decided which characteristics you want in a dog and what type of dog will best fit into your family and lifestyle. If you have selected a breeder, you have gone a step further—you have done your research and found a responsible, conscientious person who breeds quality Chow Chows and who should

BOY OR GIRL?

An important consideration to be discussed is the sex of your puppy. For a family companion, a bitch may be the better choice, considering the female's

inbred concern for all young creatures and her accompanying tolerance and patience. It is always advisable to spay a pet bitch, which may guarantee her a longer life.

be a reliable source of help as you and your puppy adjust to life together. If you have observed a litter in action, you have obtained a firsthand look at the dynamics of a puppy 'pack' and, thus, you should learn about each pup's individual personality—perhaps you have even found one that particularly appeals to you.

However, even if you have not yet found the Chow Chow puppy of your dreams, observing pups will help you learn to recognise certain behaviour and to determine what a pup's behaviour indicates about his temperament. You will be able to pick out which pups are the leaders, which ones are less outgoing, which ones are confident, which ones are shy, playful, friendly, aggressive, etc. Equally as important, you will learn to recognise what a healthy pup should look and act like. All of these things will help you in your search, and when you find the Chow Chow that was meant for you, you will know it!

Researching your breed, selecting a responsible breeder and observing as many pups as possible are all important steps on the way to dog ownership. It may seem like a lot of effort...and you have not even taken the pup home yet! Remember, though, you cannot

PUPPY PERSONALITY

When a litter becomes available to you, choosing a pup out of all those adorable faces will not be an easy task! Sound temperament is of utmost importance, but each pup has its own personality and some may be better suited to you than others. A feisty, independent pup will do well in a home with older children and adults, whilst quiet, shy puppies will thrive in a home with minimum noise and distractions. Your breeder knows the pups best and should be able to guide you in the right direction.

be too careful when it comes to deciding on the type of dog you want and finding out about your prospective pup's background. Buying a puppy is not—or should not be—just another whimsical purchase. This is one instance in which you actually do get to choose your own family! You may be thinking that buying a puppy should be fun—it should not be so serious and so much work. Keep in mind that your puppy is not a cuddly stuffed toy or decorative lawn ornament, but a creature that will become a real member of your family. You will come to realise that, while buying a puppy is a pleasurable and exciting endeavour, it is not something to be taken lightly. Relax...the fun will start when the pup comes home!

Always keep in mind that a puppy is nothing more than a baby in a furry disguise...a baby who is virtually helpless in a human world and who trusts his owner for fulfilment of his basic needs for survival. In addition to water and shelter, your pup needs care, protection, guidance and love. If you are not prepared to commit to this, then you are not prepared to own a dog.

Wait a minute, you say. How hard could this be? All of my neighbours own dogs and they seem to be doing just fine. Why

YOUR SCHEDULE . . .

If you lead an erratic, unpredictable life, with daily or weekly changes in your work requirements, consider the problems of owning a puppy. The new puppy has to be fed regularly, socialised (loved, petted, handled, introduced to other

people) and, most importantly, allowed to visit outdoors for toilet training. As the dog gets older, it can be more tolerant of deviations in its feeding and toilet relief.

DOCUMENTATION

Two important documents you will get from the breeder are the pup's pedigree and registration certificate. The breeder should register the litter and each pup with The Kennel Club, and it is necessary for you to have the paperwork if you plan on showing or breeding in the future.

Make sure you know the breeder's intentions on which type of registration he will obtain for the pup. There are limited registrations which may prohibit the dog from being shown, bred or from competing in non-conformation trials such as Working or Agility if the breeder feels that the pup is not of sufficient quality to do so. There is also a type of registration that will permit the dog in non-conformation competition only.

On the reverse side of the registration certificate, the new owner can find the transfer section which must be signed by the breeder.

should I have to worry about all of this? Well, you should not worry about it; in fact, you will probably find that once your Chow Chow pup gets used to his new home, he will fall into his place in the family quite naturally. But it never hurts to emphasise the commitment of dog ownership. With some time and patience, it is really not too difficult to raise a curious and exuberant Chow Chow pup to be a well-adjusted and well-mannered adult dog—a dog that could be your most loyal friend.

PREPARING PUPPY'S PLACE IN YOUR HOME

Researching your breed and finding a breeder are only two aspects of the 'homework' you will have to do before bringing your Chow puppy home. You will also have to prepare your home and family for the new addition. Much as you would prepare a nursery for a newborn baby, you will need to designate a place in your home that will be the puppy's own. How you prepare your home will depend on how much freedom the dog will be allowed. Whatever you decide, you must ensure that he has a place that he can 'call his own.'

DID YOU KNOW?

Many good breeders will offer you insurance with your new puppy, which is an excellent idea. The first few weeks of insurance will probably be covered free of charge or with only minimal cost, allowing you to take up the policy when this expires. If you own a pet dog, it is sensible to take out such a policy as veterinary fees can be high, although routine vaccinations and boosters are not covered. Look carefully at the many options open to you before deciding which suits you best.

DO YOUR HOMEWORK!

In order to know whether or not a puppy will fit into your lifestyle, you need to assess his personality. A good way to do this is to interact with his parents. Your pup inherits not only his appearance but also his personality and temperament from the sire and dam. If the parents are fearful or overly aggressive, these same traits may likely show up in your puppy.

When you bring your new puppy into your home, you are bringing him into what will become his home as well. Obviously, you did not buy a puppy so that he could take over your house, but in order for a puppy to grow into a stable, well-adjusted dog, he has to feel comfortable in his surroundings. Remember, he is leaving the warmth and security of his mother and littermates, as well as the familiarity of the only place he has ever known, so it is important to make his transition as easy as possible. By preparing a place in your home for the puppy, you are making him feel as welcome as possible in a strange new place. It should not take him long to get used to it, but the sudden shock of being transplanted is somewhat traumatic for a young pup. Imagine how a small child would feel in the same situation—that is how your puppy must be feeling. It is up to you to reassure him and to let him know, 'Little chap, you are going to like it here!'

INFORMATION...

Taking your dog from the breeder to your home in a car can be a very uncomfortable experience for both of you. The puppy will have been taken from his warm, friendly, safe environment and brought into a strange new environment. An environment that moves! Be prepared for loose bowels, urination, crying, whining and even fear biting. With proper love and encouragement when you arrive home, the stress of the trip should quickly disappear.

Be sure the crate you buy will be large enough for the fully grown Chow.

DID YOU KNOW?

Unfortunately, when a puppy is bought by someone who does not take into consideration the time and attention that dog ownership requires, it is the puppy who suffers when he is either abandoned or placed in a shelter by a frustrated owner. So all of the 'homework' you do in preparation for your pup's arrival will benefit you both. The more informed you are, the more you will know what to expect and the better equipped you will be to handle the ups and downs of raising a puppy. Hopefully, everyone in the household is willing to do his part in raising and caring for the pup. The anticipation of owning a dog often brings a lot of promises from excited family members: 'I will walk him every day,' 'I will feed him,' 'I will housebreak him,' etc., but these things take time and effort, and promises can easily be forgotten once the novelty of the new pet has worn off.

WHAT YOU SHOULD BUY

CRATE

To someone unfamiliar with the use of crates in dog training, it may seem like punishment to shut a dog in a crate, but this is not the case at all. Although all breeders do not advocate crate training, more and more breeders and trainers are recommending crates as a preferred tool for show puppies as well as pet puppies. Crates are not cruel—crates have many humane and highly effective uses in dog care and training. For example, crate training is a very popular and very successful housebreaking method. A crate can keep your

'YOU BETTER SHOP AROUND!'

Finding a reputable breeder that sells healthy pups is very important, but make sure that the breeder you choose is not only someone you respect but also with whom you feel comfortable. Your breeder will be a resource long after you buy your puppy, and you must be able to call with reasonable questions without being made to feel like a pest! If you don't connect on a personal level, investigate some other breeders before making a final decision.

dog safe during travel and, perhaps most importantly, a crate provides your dog with a place of his own in your home. It serves as a 'doggie bedroom' of sorts—your Chow can curl up in his crate when he wants to sleep or when he just needs a break. Many dogs sleep in their crates overnight. When lined with soft bedding and filled with his favourite toys, a crate becomes a cosy pseudo-den for your dog. Like his ancestors, he too will seek out the comfort and retreat of a den—you just happen to be providing him with something a little more luxurious than his early ancestors enjoyed.

PHOTO COURTESY OF DOSKOCIL.

Your local pet shop should have a wide variety of crates from which you can choose the crate which best suits your needs and budget.

As far as purchasing a crate, the type that you buy is up to you. It will most likely be one of the two most popular types: wire or fibreglass. There are advantages and disadvantages to each type. For example, a wire crate is more open, allowing the air to flow through and affording the dog a view of what is going on around him while a fibreglass crate is sturdier. Both can double as travel crates, providing protection for the dog. The size of the crate is another thing to consider. Puppies do not stay puppies forever—in fact, sometimes it seems as if they grow right before your eyes. A small crate may be fine for a very young Chow Chow pup, but it will not do him much good for long!

A doghouse in the garden will provide the Chow with a shady place to rest.

EXPENSE OF BREEDING

The decision to breed your dog is one that must be considered carefully and researched thoroughly before moving into action. Some people believe that breeding will make their bitch happier or that it is an easy way to make money. Unfortunately, indiscriminate breeding only worsens the rampant problem of pet overpopulation, as well as putting a considerable dent in your pocketbook. As for the bitch, the entire process from mating through whelping is not an easy one and puts your pet under considerable stress. Last, but not least, consider whether or not you have the means to care for an entire litter of pups. Without a reputation in the field, your attempts to sell the pups may be unsuccessful.

Unless you have the money and the inclination to buy a new crate every time your pup has a growth spurt, it is better to get one that will accommodate your dog both as a pup and at full size. A medium-size crate will be necessary for a full-grown Chow Chow, who stands approximately 22 inches high.

Wire crates or pens serve many useful purposes. They are lightweight and easy to carry, as they fold down and can be quickly reassembled.

BEDDING

Veterinary bedding in the dog's crate will help the dog feel more at home and you may also like to pop in a small blanket. This will take the place of the leaves, twigs, etc., that the pup would use in the wild to make a den; the pup can make his own 'burrow' in the crate. Although your pup is far removed from his den-making ancestors, the denning instinct is still a part of his genetic makeup. Second, until you bring your pup home, he has been sleeping amidst the warmth of his mother and littermates, and while a blanket is not the same as a warm, breathing body, it still provides heat and something with which to snuggle. You will want to wash your pup's bedding frequently in case he has an

You should buy a suitable crate or bed before you bring the dog home.

accident in his crate, and replace or remove any blanket that becomes ragged and starts to fall apart.

Toys

Toys are a must for dogs of all ages, especially for curious playful pups. Puppies are the 'children' of the dog world, and what child does not love toys? Chew toys provide enjoyment to both dog and owner—your dog will enjoy playing with his favourite toys, while you will enjoy the fact that they distract him from your expensive shoes and leather sofa. Puppies love to chew; in fact, chewing is a physical need for pups as they are teething, and everything looks appetising! The full range of your possessions—from old dishcloth to Oriental rug—are fair game in the eyes of a teething pup. Puppies are not all that discerning when it comes to finding something to literally 'sink their teeth into'—everything tastes great!

Chow Chow puppies are

CRATE TRAINING

During crate training, you should partition off the section of the crate in which the pup stays. If he is given too big an area, this will hinder your training efforts. Crate training is based on the fact that a dog does not like to soil his sleeping quarters, so it is ineffective to keep a pup in a crate that is so big that he can eliminate in one end and get far enough away from it to sleep. Also, you want to make the

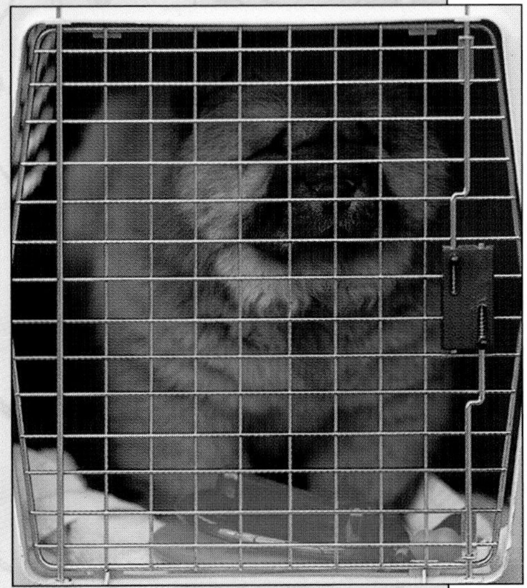

crate den-like for the pup. Blankets and a favourite toy will make the crate cosy for the small pup; as he grows, you may want to evict some of his 'roommates' to make more room.

It will take some coaxing at first, but be patient. Given some time to get used to it, your pup will adapt to his new home-within-a-home quite nicely.

Your local pet shop will have a large selection of suitable toys made especially for strong canine chewers. Never give toys made for humans to your puppy.

rather enthusiastic chewers and only the safest toys should be offered to them. Breeders advise owners to resist stuffed toys, because they can become de-stuffed in no time. The overly excited pup may ingest the stuffing, which is neither digestible nor nutritious.

Similarly, squeaky toys are quite popular, but must be avoided for the Chow Chow. Perhaps a squeaky toy can be used as an aid in training, but not for free play. If a pup 'disembowels' one of these, the small plastic squeaker inside can be dangerous if swallowed. Monitor the condition of all your pup's toys carefully and get rid of any that have been chewed to the point of becoming potentially dangerous.

Be careful of natural bones, which have a tendency to splinter into sharp, dangerous pieces. Also be careful of rawhide, which can turn into pieces that are easy to swallow and become a mushy mess on your carpet.

Lead

A nylon lead is probably the best option as it is the most resistant to puppy teeth should your pup take a liking to chewing on his lead. Of course, this is a habit that should be nipped in the bud, but if your pup likes to chew on his lead he has a very slim chance of being able to chew through the strong nylon. Nylon leads are also lightweight, which is good for a young Chow Chow who is just getting used to the idea of walking on a lead. For everyday walking and safety purposes, the nylon lead is a good choice. As your pup grows up and gets used to walking on the lead, you may want to purchase a flexible lead. These leads allow you to extend the length to give the dog a broader area to explore or to shorten the length to keep the dog closer to you.

Collar

Your pup should get used to wearing a collar all the time

MENTAL AND DENTAL

Toys not only help your puppy get the physical and mental stimulation he needs but also provide a great way to keep his teeth clean. Hard rubber or nylon toys, especially those constructed with grooves, are designed to scrape away plaque, preventing bad breath and gum infection.

TOYS, TOYS, TOYS!

With a big variety of dog toys available, and so many that look like they would be a lot of fun for a dog, be careful in your selection. It is amazing what a set of puppy teeth can do to an innocent-looking toy, so, obviously, safety is a major

consideration. Be sure to choose the most durable products that you can find. Hard nylon bones and toys are a safe bet, and many of them are offered in different scents and flavours that will be sure to capture your dog's attention. It is always fun to play a game of catch with your dog, and there are balls and flying discs that are specially made to withstand dog teeth.

The first collar and lead you buy for your Chow puppy should be very light and not overpowering.

since you will want to attach his ID tags to it. You have to attach the lead to something! A lightweight nylon collar is a good choice; make sure that it fits snugly enough so that the pup cannot wriggle out of it, but is loose enough so that it will not be uncomfortably tight around the pup's neck. You should be able to fit a finger between the pup and the collar. It may take some time for your pup to get used to wearing the collar, but soon he will not even notice that it is there. Choke collars are made for training, but should only be used by an experienced handler.

You will be able to choose from a selection of collars and leads at your local pet shop to find one that fits your Chow.

Food and Water Bowls

Your pup will need two bowls, one for food and one for water. You may want two sets of bowls, one for inside and one for outside, depending on where the dog will be fed and where he will be spending time. Stainless steel or sturdy plastic bowls are popular choices. Plastic bowls are more chewable. Dogs tend not to chew on the steel variety, which can be sterilised. It is important to buy sturdy bowls since anything is in danger of being chewed by puppy teeth and you do not want your dog to be constantly chewing apart his bowl (for his safety and for your purse!).

Cleaning Supplies

Until a pup is housetrained you will be doing a lot of cleaning. Accidents will occur, which is all right in the beginning because the puppy does not know any better. All you can do is be prepared to clean up any

CHOOSE THE PROPER COLLAR

The **BUCKLE COLLAR** is the standard collar used for everyday purpose. Be sure that you adjust the buckle on growing puppies. Check it every day. It can become too tight overnight! These collars can be made of leather or nylon. Attach your dog's identification tags to this collar.

The **CHOKE COLLAR** is the usual collar recommended for training. It is constructed of highly polished steel so that it slides easily through the stainless steel loop. The idea is that the dog controls the pressure around its neck and he will stop pulling if the collar becomes uncomfortable. Never leave a choke collar on your dog when not training.

The **HALTER** is for a trained dog that has to be restrained to prevent running away, chasing a cat and the like. Considered the most humane of all collars, it is frequently used on smaller dogs for which collars are not comfortable.

Your local pet shop will have a variety of food and water bowls from which you can choose.

Photo courtesy of Mikki Pet Products.

'accidents.' Old rags, towels, newspapers and a safe disinfectant are good to have on hand.

Beyond the Basics

The items previously discussed are the bare necessities. You will find out what else you need as you go along—grooming supplies, flea/tick protection, baby gates to partition a room, etc. These things will vary depending on your situation but it is important that you have everything you need to feed and make your Chow Chow comfortable in his first few days at home.

PUPPY-PROOFING YOUR HOME

Aside from making sure that your Chow Chow will be comfortable in your home, you also have to make sure that your home is safe for your Chow Chow. This means taking precautions that your pup will not get into anything he should not get into and that there is nothing within his reach that may harm him should he sniff it, chew it, inspect it, etc. This probably seems obvious since, while you are primarily concerned with your pup's safety, at the same time you do not want your belongings to be ruined. Breakables should be placed out of reach if your dog is to have full run of the house.

If he is to be limited to certain places within the house, keep any potentially dangerous items in the 'off-limits' areas. An electrical cord can pose a danger should the puppy decide to taste it—and who is going to convince a pup that it would not make a great chew toy? Cords should be fastened tightly against the wall. If your dog is going to spend time in a crate, make sure that there is nothing near his crate that he can reach if he sticks his curious little nose or paws through the openings. Just as you would with a child, keep all household cleaners and chemicals where the pup cannot reach them.

It is also important to make sure that the outside of your home is safe. Of course your puppy should never be unsupervised, but a pup let loose in the garden will want to run and explore, and he should be granted that freedom. Do not let a fence give you a false sense of security; you would be surprised how crafty (and persistent) a dog can be in working out how to dig under and squeeze his way through small holes, or to jump or climb over a fence. The remedy is to make the fence high enough so that it really is impossible for your dog to get over it (about 3 metres should suffice), and well embedded into the ground. Be sure to repair or secure any gaps in the fence. Check the fence periodically to ensure that it is in good shape and make repairs as needed; a very determined pup may return to the same spot to 'work on it' until he is able to get through.

TOXIC PLANTS

Many plants can be toxic to dogs. If you see your dog carrying a piece of vegetation in his mouth, approach him in a quiet, disinterested manner, avoid eye contact, pet him and gradually remove the plant from his mouth. Alternatively, offer him a treat and maybe he'll drop the plant on his own accord. Be sure no toxic plants are growing in your own garden.

Like all puppies, Chow puppies will chew on anything. Be sure to only offer him safe toys, and make certain that your home and garden are puppy-proofed.

NATURAL TOXINS

Examine your grass and garden landscaping before bringing your puppy home. Many varieties of plants have leaves, stems or flowers that are toxic if ingested, and you can depend on a curious puppy to investigate them. Ask your vet for information on poisonous plants or research them at your library.

FINANCIAL RESPONSIBILITY

Grooming tools, collars, leashes, dog beds and, of course, toys will be an expense to you when you first obtain your pup, and the cost will continue throughout your dog's lifetime. If your puppy damages or destroys your possessions (as most puppies surely will!) or something belonging to a neighbour, you can calculate additional expense. There is also flea and pest control, which every dog owner faces more than once. You must be able to handle the financial responsibility of owning a dog.

FIRST TRIP TO THE VET

You have picked out your puppy, and your home and family are ready. Now all you have to do is collect your Chow Chow from the breeder and the fun begins, right? Well...not so fast. Something else you need to prepare is your pup's first trip to the veterinary surgeon. Perhaps the breeder can recommend someone in the area that specialises in Chow Chows, or maybe you know some other Chow Chow owners who can suggest a good vet. Either way, you should have an appointment arranged for your pup before you pick him up and plan on taking him for an examination before bringing him home.

The pup's first visit will

The garden should be securely fenced, with the fence examined regularly to ensure that it is in good repair.

consist of an overall examination to make sure that the pup does not have any problems that are not apparent to the eye. The veterinary surgeon will also set up a schedule for the pup's vaccinations; the breeder will inform you of which ones the pup has already received and the vet can continue from there.

INTRODUCTION TO THE FAMILY

Everyone in the house will be excited about the puppy coming home and will want to pet him and play with him, but it is best to make the introduction low-key so as not to overwhelm the puppy. He is apprehensive already. It is the first time he has been separated from his mother and the breeder, and the ride to your home is likely to be the first time he has been in a car. The last thing you want to do is smother him, as this will only frighten him further. This is not to say that human contact is not extremely necessary at this stage, because this is the time when a connection between the pup and his human family is formed. Gentle petting and soothing words should help console him, as well as just putting him down and letting him explore on his own (under your watchful eye, of course).

The pup may approach the family members or may busy himself with exploring for a while. Gradually, each person should spend some time with the pup, one at a time, crouching down to get as close to the pup's level as possible

CHEMICAL TOXINS

Scour your garage for potential puppy dangers. Remove weed killers, pesticides and antifreeze materials. Antifreeze is highly toxic and even a few drops can kill an adult dog. The sweet taste attracts the animal, who will quickly consume it from the floor or curbside.

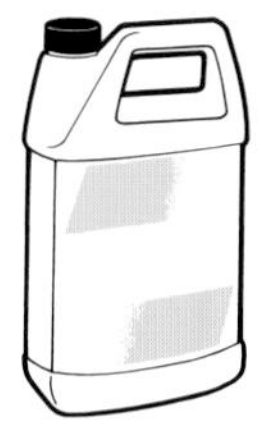

HOW VACCINES WORK

If you've just bought a puppy, you surely know the importance of having your pup vaccinated, but do you understand how vaccines work? Vaccines contain the same bacteria or viruses that cause the disease you want to prevent, but they have been chemically modified so that they don't cause any harm. Instead, the vaccine causes your dog to produce antibodies that fight the harmful bacteria. Thus, if your pup is exposed to the disease in the future, the antibodies will destroy the viruses or bacteria.

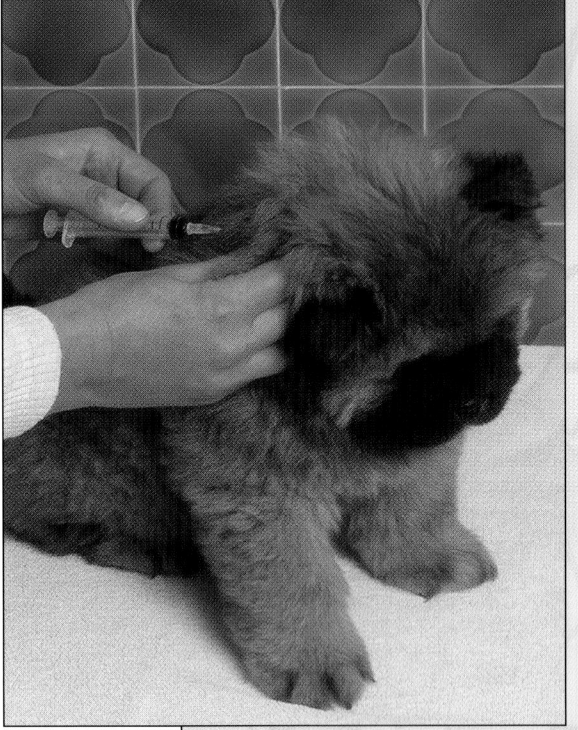

and letting him sniff their hands and petting him gently. He definitely needs human attention and he needs to be touched—this is how to form an immediate bond. Just remember that the pup is experiencing a lot of things for the first time, at the same time. There are new people, new noises, new smells, and new things to investigate: so be gentle, be affectionate, and be as comforting as you can be.

YOUR PUP'S FIRST NIGHT

You have travelled home with your new charge safely in his basket or crate. He's been to the vet for a thorough check-up; he's been weighed, his papers examined; perhaps he's even been vaccinated and wormed as well. He's met the family, licked the whole family, including the excited children and the less-than-happy cat. He's explored his area, his new bed, the garden and anywhere else he's been permitted. He's eaten his first meal at home and relieved himself in the proper place. He's heard lots of new sounds, smelled new friends and seen more of the outside world than ever before.

That was just the first day! He's worn out and is ready for bed...or so you think!

It's puppy's first night and you are ready to say 'Good

night'—keep in mind that this is puppy's first night ever to be sleeping alone. His dam and littermates are no longer at paw's length and he's a bit scared, cold and lonely. Be reassuring to your new family member. This is not the time to spoil him and give in to his inevitable whining.

Puppies whine. They whine to let others know where they are and hopefully to get company out of it. Place your pup in his new bed or crate in his room and close the door. Mercifully, he may fall asleep without a peep. If the inevitable occurs, ignore the whining: he is fine. Be strong and keep his interest in mind. Do not allow yourself to feel guilty and visit the pup. He will fall asleep eventually.

Many breeders recommend placing a piece of bedding from his former home in his new bed so that he recognises the scent of his littermates. Others still advise placing a hot water bottle in his bed for warmth. This latter may be a good idea provided the pup doesn't attempt to suckle—he'll get good and wet and may not fall asleep so fast.

Puppy's first night can be somewhat stressful for the pup and his new family. Remember that you are setting the tone of nighttime at your house. Unless

MANNERS MATTER

During the socialisation process, a puppy should meet people, experience different environments and definitely be exposed to other canines. Through playing and interacting with other dogs, your puppy will learn lessons,

ranging from controlling the pressure of his jaws by biting his litter mates to the inner-workings of the canine pack that he will apply to his human relationships for the rest of his life. That is why removing a puppy from its litter too early (before eight weeks) can be detrimental to the pup's development.

> **DID YOU KNOW?**
>
> It will take at least two weeks for your puppy to become accustomed to his new surroundings. Give him lots of love, attention, handling, frequent opportunities to relieve himself, a diet he likes to eat and a place he can call his own.

you want to play with your pup every evening at 10 p.m., midnight and 2 a.m., don't initiate the habit. Your family will thank you, and so will your pup!

PREVENTING PUPPY PROBLEMS

SOCIALISATION

Socialising your Chow Chow pup gives you the opportunity to show off your new friend, and your pup gets to reap the benefits of being an adorable furry creature that people will want to pet and, in general, think is absolutely precious!

> **PUPPY STRESS**
>
> Some experts in canine health advise that stress during a dog's early years of development can compromise and weaken his immune system and may trigger the potential for a shortened life expectancy. They emphasise the need for happy and stress-free growing-up years.

Don't overwhelm your Chow with too much too fast—Chows are not spaniels or Beagles that thrive on constant handling and attention. Chows must be convinced that human handling leads to positive rewards and will slowly warm up to new people.

Besides getting to know his new family, your puppy should be exposed to other people, animals and situations, but of course he must not come into close contact with dogs you don't know well until his course of injections is fully complete. This will help him become well adjusted as he grows up and less prone to being timid or fearful of the new things he will encounter. Your pup's socialisation began at the breeder's but now it is your responsibility to continue it. The socialisation he receives up until the age of 12 weeks is the most critical, as this is the time when he forms his impressions of the outside world. Be especially careful during the eight-to-ten-week period, also known as the fear period. The interaction he receives during this time should be gentle and reassuring. Lack of socialisation can manifest itself in fear and aggression as the dog grows up. He needs lots of human contact, affection, handling and exposure to other animals.

Once your pup has received his necessary vaccinations, feel free to take him out and about (on his lead, of course). Walk him around the neighbourhood, take him on your daily errands, let people pet him, let him meet other dogs and pets, etc. Puppies do not have to try to make friends; there will be no shortage of people who will want to introduce themselves. Just make sure that you carefully supervise each meeting. If the neighbourhood children want to say hello, for example, that is great—children and pups most often make great companions. Sometimes an excited child can unintentionally handle a pup too roughly, or an overzealous pup can playfully nip a little too hard. You want to make socialisation experiences positive ones. What a pup learns during this very formative stage will affect his attitude toward future encounters. You want your dog to be comfortable around everyone. A pup that has a bad experience with a child may grow up to be a dog that is shy around or aggressive toward children.

SOCIALISATION

Thorough socialisation includes not only meeting new people but also being introduced to new experi-

ences such as riding in the car, having his coat brushed, hearing the television, walking in a crowd—the list is endless. The more your pup experiences, and the more positive the experiences are, the less of a shock and the less frightening it will be for your pup to encounter new things.

Consistency in Training

Dogs, being pack animals, naturally need a leader, or else they try to establish dominance in their packs. When you bring a dog into your family, the choice of who becomes the leader and who becomes the 'pack' is entirely up to you! Your pup's intuitive quest for dominance, coupled with the

FEEDING TIPS

You will probably start feeding your pup the same food that he has been getting from the breeder; the breeder should give you a few days' supply to start you off.

Although you should not give your pup too many treats, you will want to have puppy treats on hand for coaxing, training, rewards, etc. Be careful, though, as a small pup's calorie requirements are relatively low and a few treats can add up to almost a full day's worth of calories without the required nutrition.

fact that it is nearly impossible to look at an adorable furry Chow Chow pup and not cave in, giving the pup almost an unfair advantage in getting the upper paw! A pup will definitely test the waters to see what he can and cannot do. Do not give in to those pleading eyes—stand your ground when it comes to disciplining the pup and make sure that all family members do the same. It will only confuse the pup when Mother tells him to get off the sofa when he is used to sitting up there with Father to watch the nightly news. Avoid discrepancies by having all members of the household decide on the rules before the pup even comes home...and be consistent in enforcing them! Early training shapes the dog's personality, so you cannot be unclear in what you expect.

COMMON PUPPY PROBLEMS

The best way to prevent puppy problems is to be proactive in stopping an undesirable behaviour as soon as it starts. The old saying 'You can't teach an old dog new tricks' does not necessarily hold true, but it is true that it is much easier to discourage bad behaviour in a young developing pup than to wait until the pup's bad behaviour becomes the adult

PUPPY PROBLEMS

The majority of problems that are commonly seen in young pups will disappear as your dog gets older. However, how you deal with problems when he is young will determine how he reacts to discipline as an adult dog. It is important to establish who is boss (hopefully it will be you!) right away when you are first bonding with your dog. This bond will set the tone for the rest of your life together.

dog's bad habit. There are some problems that are especially prevalent in puppies as they develop.

Nipping

As puppies start to teethe, they feel the need to sink their teeth into anything available...unfortunately that includes your fingers, arms, hair and toes. You may find this behaviour cute for the first five seconds...until you feel just how sharp those puppy teeth are. This is something you want to discourage immediately and consistently with a firm 'No!' (or whatever number of firm 'No's' it takes for him to understand that you mean business). Then replace your finger with an appropriate chew toy. While this behaviour is merely annoying when the dog is young, it can become dangerous as your Chow Chow's adult teeth grow in and his jaws develop, and he continues to think it is okay to gnaw on human appendages. Your Chow Chow does not mean any harm with a friendly nip, but he also does not know his own strength.

CHEWING TIPS

Chewing goes hand in hand with nipping in the sense that a teething puppy is always looking for a way to soothe his aching gums. In this case, instead of chewing on you, he may have taken a liking to your favourite shoe or something else which he should not be chewing. Again, realise that this is a normal canine behaviour that does not need to be discouraged, only redirected. Your pup just needs to be taught what is acceptable to chew on and what is off limits. Consistently tell him NO when you catch him chewing on something forbidden and give him a chew toy. Conversely, praise him when you catch him chewing on something appropriate. In this way you are discouraging the inappropriate behaviour and reinforcing the desired behaviour. The puppy chewing should stop after his adult teeth have come in, but an adult dog continues to chew for various reasons—perhaps because he is bored, perhaps to relieve tension or perhaps he just likes to chew. That is why it is important to redirect his chewing when he is still young.

Crying/Whining

Your pup will often cry, whine, whimper, howl or make some type of commotion when he is left alone. This is basically his way of calling out for attention to make sure that you know he is there and that you have not

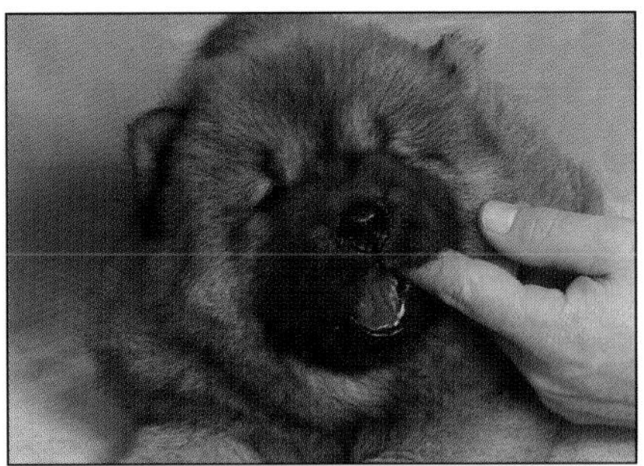

A finger makes a tasty treat for a teething pup! Nipping, however, should be discouraged as it can lead to dangerous habits as the dog matures.

forgotten about him. He feels insecure when he is left alone, when you are out of the house and he is in his crate or when you are in another part of the house and he cannot see you. The noise he is making is an expression of the anxiety he feels at being alone, so he needs to be taught that being alone is okay. You are not actually training the dog to stop making noise, you are training him to feel comfortable when he is alone and thus removing the need for him to make the noise. This is where the crate filled with cosy bedding and a toy comes in handy. You want to know that he is safe when you are not there to supervise, and you know that he will be safe in his crate rather than roaming freely about the house. In order for the pup to stay in his crate without making a fuss, he needs to be comfortable in his crate. On that note, it is extremely important that the crate is never used as a form of punishment, or the pup will have a negative association with the crate.

Accustom the pup to the crate in short, gradually increasing time intervals in which you put him in the crate, maybe with a treat, and stay in the room with him. If he cries or makes a fuss, do not go to him, but stay in his sight. Gradually he will realise that staying in his crate is all right without your help, and it will not be so traumatic for him when you are not around. You may want to leave the radio on softly when you leave the house; the sound of human voices may be comforting to him.

PLAY'S THE THING

Teaching the puppy to play with his toys in running and fetching games is an ideal way to help the puppy develop muscle, learn motor skills and bond with you his owner and master.

He also needs to learn how to inhibit his bite reflex and never to use his teeth on people, forbidden objects and other animals in play. Whenever you play with your puppy, you make the rules. This becomes an important message to your puppy in teaching him that you are the pack leader and control everything he does in life. Once your dog accepts you as his leader, your relationship with him will be cemented for life.

EVERYDAY CARE OF YOUR CHOW CHOW

FEEDING YOUR CHOW CHOW

When you take your puppy home, it is normally around eight weeks of age, should have been carefully weaned, and will perhaps be on three meals per day. Whether you fully agree with the breeder's diet and feeding regimen, it is inadvisable to make sudden changes. After all, it will not have been so long since your puppy was feeding from its mother and will only have been weaned for perhaps three weeks. Your breeder will know which food is best suited, and how much is needed. If, at some time, you need or decide to make changes in the pup's diet, then the change should always be administered with the greatest care, and without haste. It is normal practice for caring breeders to advise on all aspects of the puppy's lifestyle, and they will invariably let you know what food to obtain beforehand. Some will actually ensure that there is some ready for you to take home. In days gone by, when plenty of fresh meat was obtainable at reasonable prices, we would normally feed that, mixed with some good-quality biscuit meal. In more recent times, with restrictions on the production and retailing of fresh meat, more dog owners have moved over to the complete foods, while some prefer tins. The former comes in flake or pellet form, preferably moistened. If a dog was living

DO DOGS HAVE TASTE BUDS?

Watching a dog 'wolf' or gobble his food, seemingly without chewing, leads an owner to wonder whether

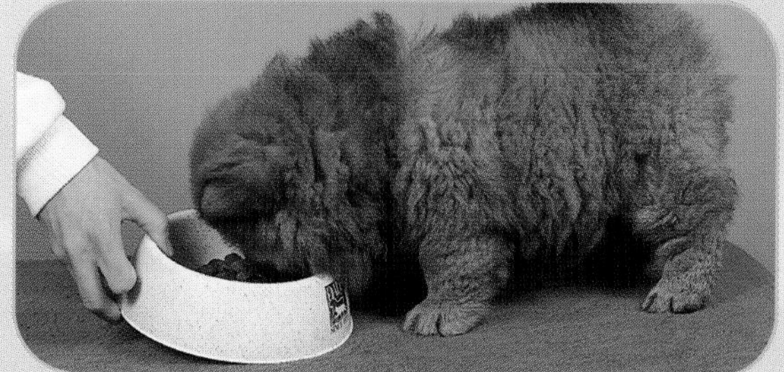

their dogs can taste anything. Yes, dogs have taste buds, with sensory perception of sweet, salty and sour. Puppies are born with fully mature taste buds.

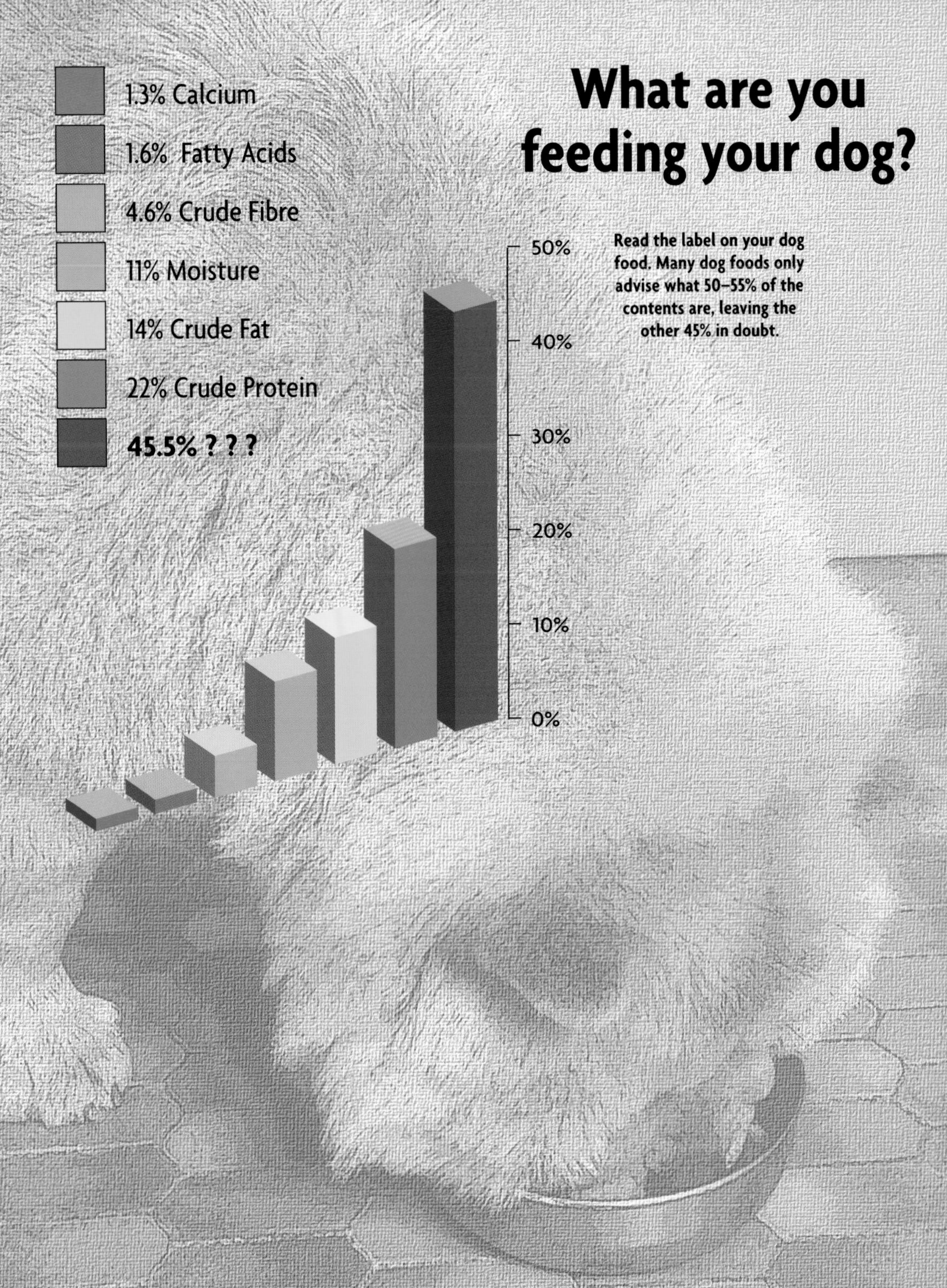
1.3% Calcium
1.6% Fatty Acids
4.6% Crude Fibre
11% Moisture
14% Crude Fat
22% Crude Protein
45.5% ? ? ?
What are you feeding your dog?
50%
40%
30%
20%
10%
0%
Read the label on your dog food. Many dog foods only advise what 50–55% of the contents are, leaving the other 45% in doubt.

wild, the food that it hunted would not be in a dry form, therefore I feel it is unfair to expect our dogs' digestions to adapt to unnatural nutrition.

When considering the purchase of any breed, the cost of feeding is something that should be taken into account. A growing dog will gradually need larger quantities, even though the number of feedings will eventually be reduced to one per day. We always fed our puppies a cereal-type breakfast, a light lunch and an evening meat and meal mixture. Today's complete foods are carefully formulated and will be graded according to needs: puppy, junior, adult, senior, etc. They are sold with details of amounts required according to size of breed and any preparation needs. The grading ensures that the balance of protein and carbohydrate is in keeping with growth stages.

Puppy Stage

Puppies instinctively want to suck milk from their mother's teats and a normal puppy will exhibit this behaviour from just a few moments following birth. If puppies do not attempt to suckle within the first half-hour or so, they should be encouraged to do so by placing them on the nipples, having selected ones with plenty of milk. This early milk supply is important in providing colostrum to protect the puppies during the first eight to ten weeks of their lives. Although a mother's milk is much better than any milk formula, despite there being some excellent ones available, if the puppies do not feed you will have to feed them yourself. For those with less experience, advice from a veterinary surgeon is important so that you feed not only the right quantity of milk but that of correct quality, fed at suitably frequent intervals, usually every two hours during the first few days of life.

There is nothing more nourishing and beneficial than mother's milk for newborn puppies.

Puppies should be allowed to nurse from their mothers for about the first six weeks, although from the third or fourth week you will have begun to introduce small portions of suitable solid food.

> **CHANGE IN DIET**
>
> As your dog's caretaker, you know the importance of keeping his diet consistent, but sometimes when you run out of food or if you're on holiday, you have to make a change quickly. Some dogs will experience digestive problems but most will not. If you are planning on changing your dog's menu, do so gradually to ensure that your dog will not have any problems. Over a period of four to five days, slowly add some new food to your dog's old food, increasing the percentage of new food each day.

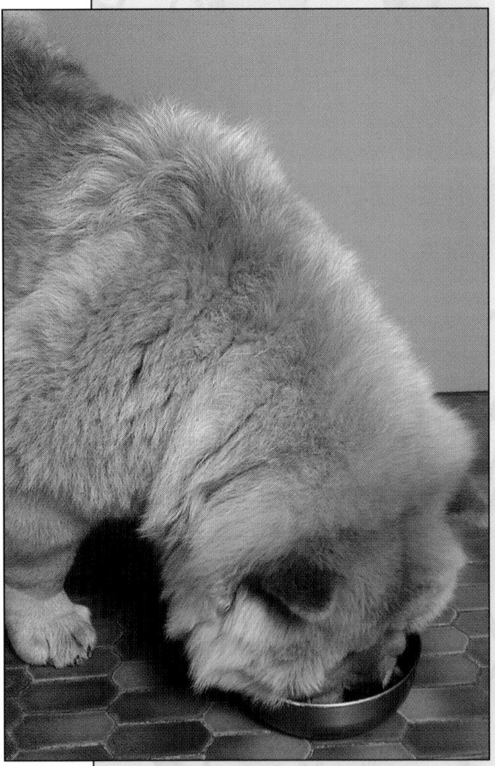

Most breeders like to introduce alternate milk and meat meals initially, building up to weaning time.

By the time the puppies are seven or a maximum of eight weeks old, they should be fully weaned and fed solely on a proprietary puppy food. Selection of the most suitable, good-quality diet at this time is essential for a puppy's fastest growth rate is during the first year of life. Veterinary surgeons are usually able to offer advice in this regard and, although the frequency of meals will have been reduced over time, only when a young dog has reached the age of about 12 months should an adult diet be fed.

Puppy and junior diets should be well balanced for the needs of your dog, so that except in certain circumstances additional vitamins, minerals and proteins will not be required.

Adult Diets

A dog is considered an adult when it has stopped growing, so in general the diet of a Chow can be changed to an adult one at about 10 to 12 months of age. Again you should rely upon your veterinary surgeon or dietary specialist to recommend an acceptable maintenance diet. Major dog food manufacturers specialise in this type of food, and it is merely necessary for you to select the one best suited to your dog's needs. Active dogs may have different requirements than sedate dogs.

SENIOR DIETS

As a dog gets older, his metabolism changes. The older dog usually exercises less, moves more slowly and sleeps more. This change in lifestyle and physiological performance requires a change in diet. Since these changes take place slowly, they might not be recognisable. What is easily recognisable is weight gain. By continuing to feed your dog an adult-maintenance diet when it is slowing down metabolically, your dog will gain weight. Obesity in an older dog compounds the health problems that already accompany old age.

As your dog gets older, few of his organs function up to par. The kidneys slow down and the intestines become less efficient. These age-related factors are best handled with a change in diet and a change in feeding schedule to give smaller portions that are more easily digested.

There is no single best diet for every older dog. While many dogs do well on light or senior diets, other dogs do better on puppy diets or other special premium diets such as lamb and rice. Be sensitive to your senior Chow's diet and this will help control other problems that may arise with your old friend.

'DOES THIS COLLAR MAKE ME LOOK FAT?'

Whilst humans may obsess about how they look and how trim their bodies are, many people believe that extra weight on their dogs is a good thing. The truth is, pets should not be over- or under-weight, as both can lead to or signal sickness. In order to tell how fit your pet is, run your hands over his ribs. Are his ribs buried under a layer of fat or are they sticking out considerably? If your pet is

within his normal weight range, you should be able to feel the ribs easily. If you stand above him, the outline of his body should resemble an hourglass. Some breeds do tend to be leaner; while some are a bit stockier, but making sure your dog is the right weight for his breed will certainly contribute to his good health.

WATER

Just as your dog needs proper nutrition from his food, water is an essential 'nutrient' as well.

Daily walks are equally beneficial for dogs and their owners.

Water keeps the dog's body properly hydrated and promotes normal function of the body's systems. During housebreaking it is necessary to keep an eye on how much water your Chow is drinking, but once he is reliably trained he should have access to clean fresh water at all times, especially if you feed dried food. Make sure that the dog's water bowl is clean, and change the water often.

EXERCISE

The Chow Chow who is involved in the family activities is twice blessed. Providing the Chow with active participation in outdoor endeavours allows for exercise as well as social stimulation. The best exercise for a Chow involves his owner, other members of the family or familiar friends. The Chow cannot be permitted to lead a sedentary lifestyle. Not only is this unhealthy for any dog, but for a Chow, lack of exercise and social outings makes him a

All Chows, puppies and adults, must always have fresh, clean water available.

recluse, totally disinterested in other life forms. Many Chows are self-sufficient and aloof, rarely looking for company and play.

Exercise and play are vital to all dogs, and the Chow is a special case indeed. Regular walks, fetching balls in the garden, or letting the dog run free in the garden under your supervision are excellent outings for the Chow. For those who are more ambitious, you will find that your Chow also enjoys long walks, an occasional hike or a trip to the beach. Family picnics, dog show weekends, road trips and the like are ideal as they offer the Chow opportunities to engage in social exchanges, ever increasing the dog's ability to 'let his ruff down' and let his charming leonine personality 'roar'!

Bear in mind that an overweight dog should never be suddenly over-exercised; instead he should be allowed to increase exercise slowly. Not only is exercise essential to keep the dog's body fit, it is essential to his mental well-being. A bored dog will find something to do, which often manifests itself in some type of destructive behaviour. In this sense, exercise is essential for the owner's mental well-being as well!

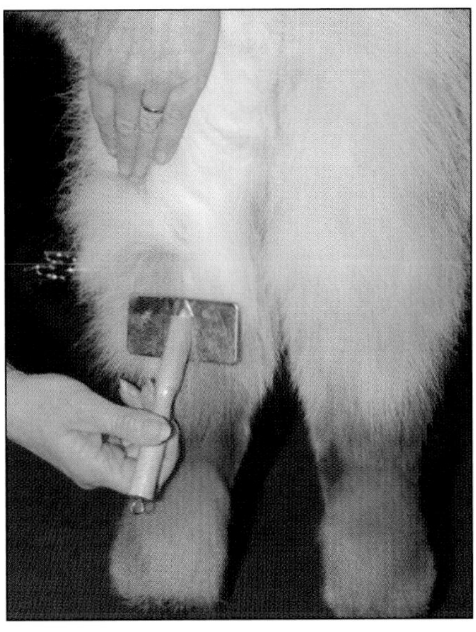

The Chow is a natural breed, meaning that its coat needs no special clipping or trimming. Regular brushing is enough to keep the Chow's coat in good condition.

GROOMING

It is important to remember that the Chow is a natural breed that requires no clipping or trimming outside of tidying up its feet or removing the whiskers. Breeders are most adamant that the Chow not fall into any grooming fads of any kind. Proper brushing is all the grooming that your Chow will ever need.

Puppy Coat

Undoubtedly the breeder from whom you bought your Chow will have begun to accustom the puppy to grooming as soon as there was enough hair to brush. You must continue with grooming sessions or begin them at once if for some reason they have not been started. You

DRINK, DRANK, DRUNK—MAKE IT A DOUBLE

In both humans and dogs, as well as most living organisms, water forms the major part of nearly every body tissue. Naturally, we take water for granted, but without it, life as we know it would cease.

For dogs, water is needed to keep their bodies functioning biochemically. Additionally, water is needed to replace the water lost while panting. Unlike humans who are able to sweat to dissipate heat, dogs must pant to cool down, thereby losing the vital water from their bodies needed to regulate their body temperatures. Humans lose electrolyte-containing products and other body-fluid components through sweating; dogs do not lose anything except water.

Water is essential always, but especially so when the weather is hot or humid or when your dog is exercising or working vigorously.

and your Chow will spend many hours involved with this activity over a lifetime, so it is imperative you both learn to cooperate in the endeavour to make it an easy and pleasant experience.

The first piece of equipment you will have to obtain is a grooming table. A grooming table can be built or purchased at your local pet shop. Make sure the table is of a height at which you can work comfortably either sitting or standing. Adjustable-height grooming tables are available at most pet shops. Although you will buy this when your Chow puppy first arrives, anticipate its full-grown size in making your purchase and select or build a table that will accommodate a fully grown Chow lying on its side.

You will also need to invest in two brushes, a steel comb, barber's scissors and a pair of nail clippers. For the finish work you will need a commercial coat conditioner and a spray bottle. Consider the fact you will be using this equipment for many years so buy the best of these items that you can afford.

The two brushes that you will need are: a wire 'slicker brush' (also called a 'rake') and a pin brush (sometimes called a 'Poodle brush').

PROPER DIET TESTING

A good test for proper diet is the colour, odour and firmness of your dog's stool. A healthy dog usually produces three semi-hard stools per day. The stools should have no unpleasant odour. They should be the same colour from excretion to excretion.

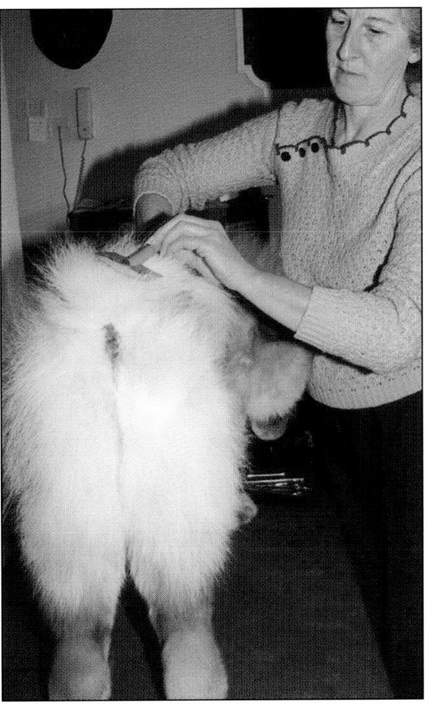

Hair should be brushed in the direction in which it falls. With the Chow, the hair on the tail naturally curls over the back.

Do not attempt to groom your Chow on the floor. The puppy will only attempt to get away from you when it has decided enough is enough, and you will spend a good part of your time chasing the puppy around the room. Nor is sitting on the floor for long stretches of time the most comfortable position in the world for the average adult.

The Chow puppy must be taught to lie on its side to be groomed. It will be kept in that position for most of the grooming process. The puppy will also have to be kept in the sitting and standing position, but the lying position takes the most time and is more difficult for the puppy to learn. The Chow trained to lie quietly on its side will prove to be a true godsend when the dog is grown and has developed a mature coat.

Begin this training by picking the puppy up as you

GROOMING EQUIPMENT

How much grooming equipment you purchase will depend on how much grooming you are going to do. Here are some basics:

- Natural bristle brush
- Slicker brush
- Metal comb
- Scissors
- Blaster
- Rubber mat
- Dog shampoo
- Spray hose attachment
- Ear cleaner
- Cotton wipes
- Towels
- Nail clippers

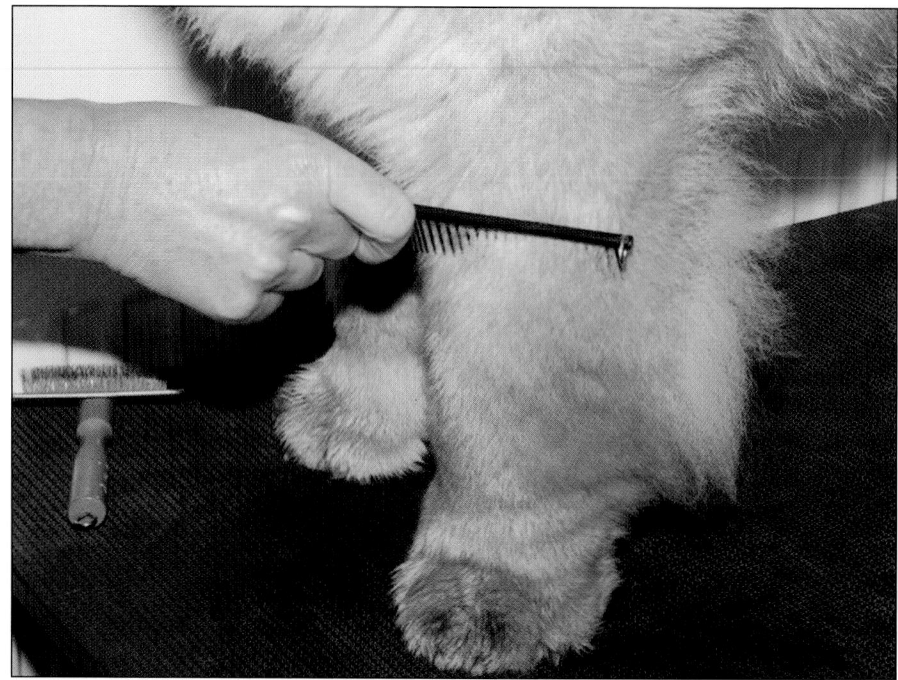

Shorter hair on the Chow's legs can be sufficiently maintained with a metal comb.

would a lamb with its side against your chest and your arms wrapped around the puppy's body. Lay the puppy down on the table, release your arms but keep your chest pressed lightly down on the puppy's side. Speak reassuringly to the Chow, stroking its head and rump. (This is a good time to practise the 'Stay' command.) Do this a number of times before you attempt to do any grooming. Repeat the process until your puppy understands what it is supposed to do when you place it on the grooming table.

Start with the slicker brush and begin what is called 'line-brushing' at the top of the shoulder. Part the hair in a straight line from the front of the shoulder straight on down to the bottom of the chest. Brush through the hair to the right and left of the part, lightly spraying the area with the coat conditioner as you go. Start at the skin and brush out to the very end of the hair. Do a small section at a time and continue on down the part. When you reach the bottom of the part, return to the top and make another part just to the right of the first line you brushed. Part, brush and spray. You will repeat this process working toward the rear until you reach the puppy's tail.

I prefer to do the legs on the same side I have been working on at this time. Use the same process, parting the hair at the top of the leg and working down. Do this all around the leg and be especially careful to attend to the hard-to-reach areas under the upper legs where they join the body. Mats occur in these areas very rapidly, especially during the time when the Chow is casting its puppy coat.

Should you encounter a mat that does not brush out easily, use your fingers and the steel comb to separate the hairs as much as possible. Do not cut or pull out the matted hair. Apply baby powder or one of the specially prepared grooming powders directly to the mat and brush completely from the skin out.

When you have finished the legs on the one side, turn the puppy over and complete the entire process, on the other side—part, spray, brush. As your Chow becomes accustomed to this process, you may find the puppy considers this nap time. You may have to lift your puppy into sitting position to arouse it from its slumber.

While the puppy is sitting, you can do the hair of the chest using the line-brushing method here as well. Next stand the puppy up and do the tail. Check the longer hair of the 'pants' on the rear legs to make sure they are thoroughly brushed, especially around the area of the anus and genitalia. Needless to say, it is important to be extremely careful when brushing in these areas in that they are extremely sensitive and easily injured.

When the line-brushing process is completed, it is time for the finishing touches. Use your barber scissors to trim any long or shaggy hairs around the Chow's feet. The Chow's foot should be round and compact looking. You may trim off your Chow's whiskers if you wish.

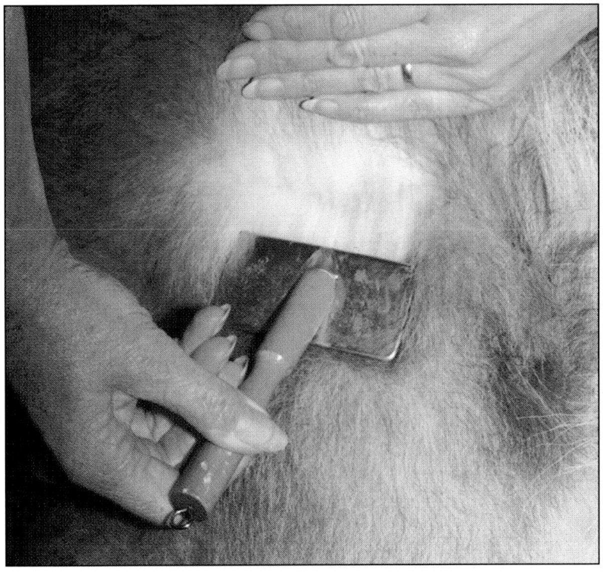

Learn the correct way to brush your Chow's coat and make regular grooming a habit.

GROOMING TIP

Although grooming the pet Chow might seem like a daunting task, it is possible to do it

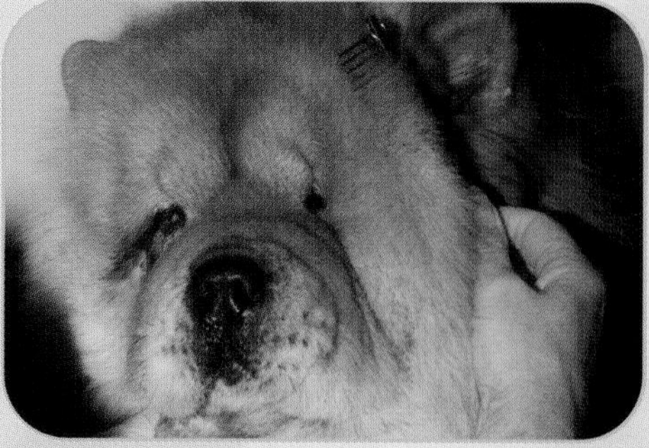

yourself. Watch a professional work on your dog a few times and then practise yourself.

This is optional, however. Many Chow owners prefer to leave the whiskers on.

Brush the hair around the head, shoulders and on the back forward. Do the same with the hair on the tail. Brush the chest hair downward and do the same with the hair on the sides of the dog.

This is also a good time to accustom your Chow to having its nails trimmed and having its feet inspected. Always inspect your dog's feet for cracked pads. Check between the toes for splinters and thorns. Pay particular attention to any swollen or tender areas. In many sections of the world, there is a weed called a 'fishtail' that has a barbed hook-like affair that carries its seed. This hook easily finds its way into a Chow's foot or between its toes and very quickly works its way deep into the dog's flesh. This will very quickly cause soreness and infection. Fishtails are best removed by your vet before serious problems develop.

The nails of a Chow who spends most of its time indoors or on grass when outdoors can grow long very quickly. Do not allow the nails to become overgrown and then expect to cut them back easily. Each nail has a blood vessel running through the centre called the 'quick.' The quick grows close

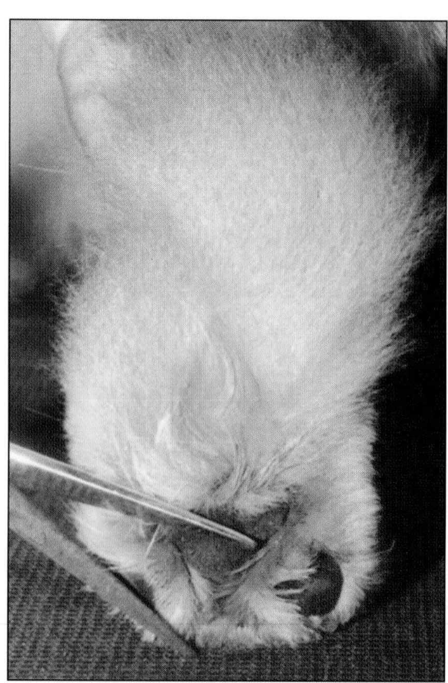

Scissoring around the Chow's feet to give them a neat look is about all the trimming that the Chow's coat requires.

to the end of the nail and contains very sensitive nerve endings. If the nail is allowed to grow too long, it will be impossible to cut it back to a proper length without cutting into the quick. This causes severe pain to the dog and can also result in a great deal of bleeding that can be very difficult to stop.

If your Chow is getting plenty of exercise on cement or rough, hard pavement, the nails may keep sufficiently worn down. Otherwise the nails can grow long very quickly. They must then be trimmed with canine nail clippers, an electric nail grinder (also called a drummel) or coarse file made expressly for that purpose. All three of these items can be purchased at well-stocked pet shops.

The electric nail grinder is preferred above the others because it is so easy to control and helps avoid cutting into the quick. The Chow's dark nails make it practically impossible to see where the quick ends, so regardless of which nail trimming device is used, one must proceed with caution and remove only a small portion of the nail at time.

Use of the electric grinder requires introducing your puppy to it at an early age. The instrument has a whining sound

With black or dark nails, where the quick is not easy to see, it's best to clip only the tip of the nail or to use a file.

In light-coloured nails, clipping is much simpler because you can see the vein (or quick) that grows inside the casing.

Your local pet shop can supply you with suitable nail clippers. Start the nail clipping routine when your Chow is a puppy.

to it not unlike a dentist's drill. The noise combined with the vibration of the sanding head on the nail itself can take some getting used to, but most dogs I have used it on eventually accept it as one of life's trials. Most dogs do not like having their nails trimmed no matter which device is used so my own eventual decision was to use the grinder, as I was less apt to damage the quick.

Should the quick be nipped in the trimming process, there are any number of blood-clotting products available that will almost immediately stem the flow of blood. It is wise to have one of these products on hand in case there is a nail-trimming accident or the dog tears a nail on its own.

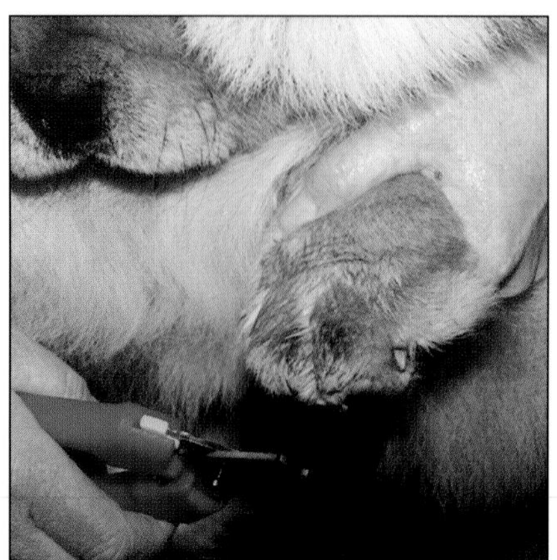

Adult nails will be thicker than puppy nails and will require a stronger clipper.

Grooming the Adult Chow

Fortunately, you and your Chow have spent the many months between puppyhood and full maturity learning to assist each other through the grooming process. The two of you have survived the casting of the puppy coat and the arrival of the entirely different adult hair. Not only is the Chow's adult hair of an entirely different texture, it is much longer and much thicker.

Undoubtedly by this time you have realised the pin brush with its longer bristles set in rubber is far more effective for line-brushing the adult Chow than the slicker brush that you used through puppyhood. The method of brushing the adult coat is the same as that used since your Chow was a puppy. The obvious difference is that you have more dog and more hair.

While one might expect grooming an adult Chow to be a monumental task, this is not necessarily so. The two of you have been practising the brushing routine for so long it has undoubtedly become second nature to both of you. The coarseness of the adult Chow's hair is actually much easier to cope with than was the puppy coat. The ease of working with the Chow's adult coat plus your own experience in the grooming routine combine to make the task far easier than what one might expect. Ten industriously applied minutes a day with a brush, in addition to a thorough weekly session, will keep your Chow looking in the best of shape.

On the other hand, if the coat is neglected and becomes matted, you will indeed have a difficult time ahead of you. The coat can become 'felted' with mats and you may have to resort to having a vet or groomer shave the matted-to-the-skin Chow. This should be resorted to only under extreme circumstances. Some misguided owners feel they are doing their dog a service by shaving the coat in summer when exactly the opposite is true. The Chow's coat serves as insulation against both heat and cold.

NAIL MAINTENANCE

A dog that spends a lot of time outside on a hard surface, such as cement or pavement, will have his nails naturally worn down and may not need to have them trimmed as often, except maybe in the colder months when he is not outside as much. Regardless, it is best to get your dog accustomed to this procedure at an early age so that he is used to it. Some dogs are especially sensitive about having their feet touched, but if a dog has experienced it since he was young, he should not be bothered by it.

BATHING

Following the proper coat care procedure will all but eliminate the need for bathing a Chow. Dog show exhibitors use coat care products that adhere to the

BATHING TIP

The use of human soap products like shampoo, bubble bath and hand soap can be damaging to a dog's coat and skin. Human products are too strong and remove the protective oils coating the dog's hair and skin (making him water-resistant). Use only shampoo made especially for dogs and you may like to use a medicated shampoo, which will always help to keep external parasites at bay.

Chow's hair and may make bathing necessary on occasion. Even at that, most Chow exhibitors use 'dry bath' products rather than the tub and shampoo method. Well-kept Chows are literally odour-free and frequent bathing serves little purpose. Bathing can dry out the Chow's skin and hair creating unnecessary problems.

If you must bath your Chow never bath it while matted. Wetting the matted hair will only complicate the situation and the end result will provide you with much more work than if you had completed the mat-removal process prior to bathing. On the rare occasions your Chow requires a wet bath, you will need to gather the necessary equipment ahead of time.

A rubber mat should be placed at the bottom of the tub to avoid your Chow's slipping and thereby becoming frightened. A rubber spray hose is absolutely necessary to thoroughly wet the Chow's dense coat. The hose is also necessary to remove all shampoo residue.

A small piece of cotton placed inside each ear will avoid water running down into the dog's ear canal and a drop or two of mineral oil or a dab of petroleum jelly placed in each eye will preclude shampoo irritating the Chow's eyes.

It is best to use a shampoo designed especially for dogs. The pH balance is adjusted to keep drying to a minimum and leaves the hair shining and lustrous.

BATHING TIP

Once you are sure that the dog is thoroughly rinsed, squeeze the excess water out of the coat with your hand and dry him with a heavy towel. You may choose to use a blaster on his coat or just let it dry naturally. In cold weather, never allow your dog outside with a wet coat.

There are 'dry bath' products on the market, which are sprays and powders intended for spot cleaning, that can be used between regular baths, if necessary. They are not substitutes for regular baths, but they are easy to use for touch-ups as they do not require rinsing.

In bathing, start behind the ears and work back. Use a face flannel to soap and rinse around the head and face. Once you have shampooed your Chow, you must rinse the coat thoroughly and when you feel quite certain all shampoo residue has been removed, rinse once more. Shampoo residue in the coat is sure to dry the hair and could cause skin irritation.

As soon as you have completed the bath, use heavy towels to remove as much of the excess water as possible. Your Chow will assist you in the process by shaking a great deal of the water out of its coat on its own.

Before your Chow is completely dry, it is best to brush out the coat to avoid mats and tangles from forming. Use the same brushing process you normally use.

My advice is to avoid the wet bath unless it is absolutely necessary. There are so many effective dry bath products available that the time-consuming wet bath need only be resorted to in extreme circumstances.

Ear Cleaning

The ears should be kept clean and any excess hair inside the ear should be carefully removed. Ears can be cleaned with a cotton wipe and ear

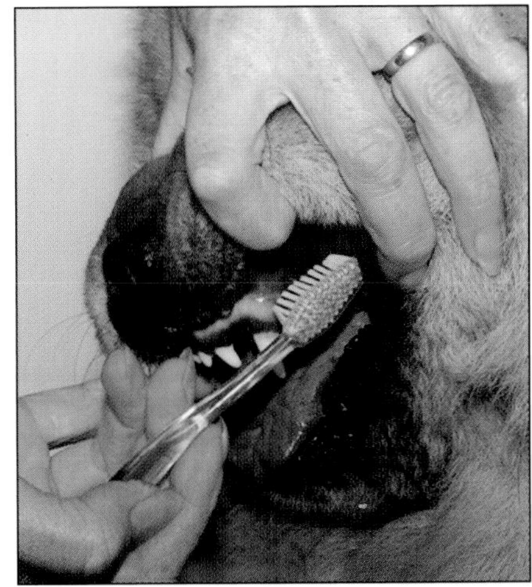

Part of good grooming is brushing your dog's teeth.

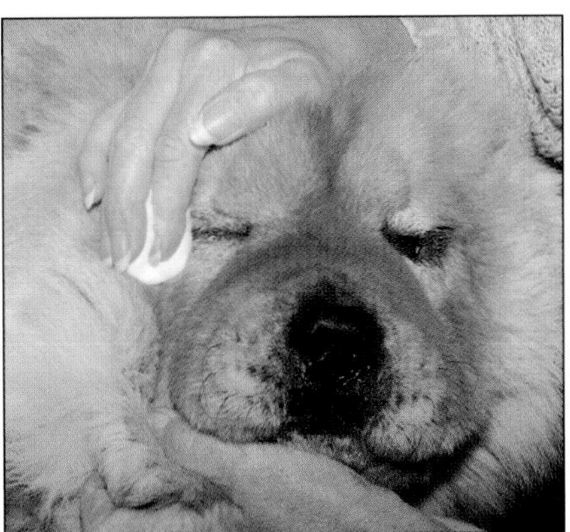

The areas around the eyes can be wiped with a special cleaner formulated for dogs.

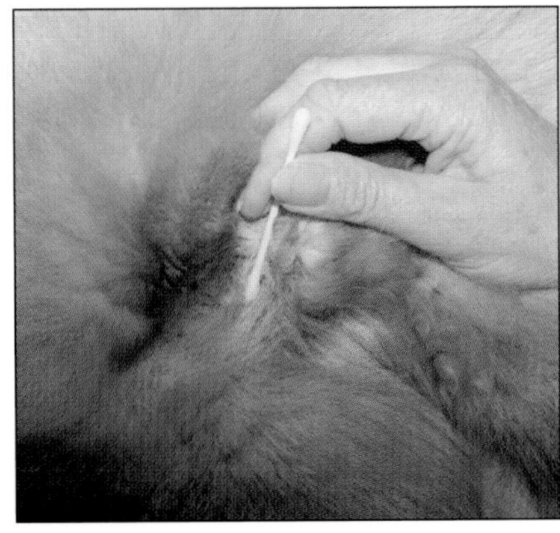

Your Chow's ears should be cleaned very carefully. Probing with a cotton bud is not advised; a cotton wipe is much safer.

TRAVEL TIP

When travelling, never let your dog off-lead in a strange area. Your dog could run away out of fear or decide to chase a passing squirrel or cat or simply want to stretch his legs without restriction—you might never see your canine friend again.

MOTION SICKNESS

*If life is a motorway...*your dog may not want to come along for the ride! Some dogs experience motion sickness in cars that leads to excessive salivation and even vomiting. In most cases, your dog will fare better in the familiar, safe confines of his crate. To desensitise your dog, try going on several short jaunts before trying a long trip. If your dog experiences distress when riding in the vehicle, drive with him only when absolutely necessary, and do not feed him or give him water before you go.

TRAVEL TIP

If you are going on a long motor trip with your dog, be sure the hotels are dog friendly. Many hotels do not accept dogs. Also take along some ice that can be thawed and offered to your dog if he becomes overheated. Most dogs like to lick ice.

powder made especially for dogs. Be on the lookout for any signs of infection or ear mite infestation. If your Chow has been shaking his head or scratching at his ears frequently, this usually indicates a problem. If his ears have an unusual odour, this is a sure sign of mite infestation or infection, and a signal to have his ears checked by the veterinary surgeon.

TRAVELLING WITH YOUR DOG

Car Travel

You should accustom your Chow to riding in a car at an early age. You may or may not take him in the car often, but at the very least he will need to go to the vet and you do not want these trips to be traumatic for the dog or troublesome for you. The safest way for a dog to ride in the car is in his crate. If he

Your Chow must be transported in his crate or cage. Never allow the dog to roam free in the car while travelling. Imagine the turmoil if you have to stop short?

uses a crate in the house, you can use the same crate for travel.

Put the pup in the crate and see how he reacts. If he seems uneasy, you can have a passenger hold him on his lap while you drive. Another option is a specially made safety harness for dogs, which straps the dog in much like a seat belt. Do not let the dog roam loose in the vehicle—this is very dangerous! If you should stop short, your dog can be thrown and injured. If the dog starts climbing on you and pestering you while you are driving, you will not be able to concentrate on the road. It is an unsafe situation for everyone—human and canine.

For long trips, be prepared to stop to let the dog relieve himself. Bring along whatever you need to clean up after him. You should also take along some paper kitchen towels and perhaps some old towelling for use should he have an accident in the car or suffer from travel sickness.

Air Travel

While it is possible to take a dog on a flight within Britain,

FREE AT LAST!

Whilst running off lead may be great fun for your dog, it can turn into a time when your dog shows you everything you did wrong in obedience class. If you want to give your dog a chance to have some fun and exercise without

the constraints of a leash, the best place to do this is in a designated fenced-in area where dogs can socialise and work off excess energy. When visiting such an area, don't let your dog run amok or unattended, watch other dogs that are present, and follow all rules, specifically those regarding waste disposal.

this is fairly unusual and advance permission is always required. The dog will be required to travel in a fibreglass crate and you should always check in advance with the airline regarding specific requirements. To help the dog be at ease, put one of his favourite toys in the crate with him. Do not feed the dog for at least six hours before the trip to minimise his need to relieve himself. However, certain regulations specify that water must always be made available to the dog in the crate.

Make sure your dog is properly identified and that your contact information appears on his ID tags and on his crate. Animals travel in a different area of the plane than human passengers so every rule must be strictly adhered to so as to prevent the risk of getting separated from your dog.

BOARDING

So you want to take a family holiday—and you want to include all members of the family. You would probably make arrangements for accommodation ahead of time anyway, but this is especially important when travelling with a dog. You do not want to make an overnight stop at the only place around for miles and find out that they do not allow dogs. Also, you do not want to reserve a place for your family without confirming that you are travelling with a dog because if it is against their policy you may not have a place to stay.

Alternatively, if you are travelling and choose not to bring your Chow, you will have to make arrangements for him while you are away. Some options are to take him to a neighbour's house to stay while you are gone, to have a trusted

There are kennels available to board your Chow if you cannot take him along on your trip. Visit several kennels and choose one before you actually require its services.

neighbour stop by often or stay at your house, or bring your dog to a reputable boarding kennel. If you choose to board him at a kennel, you should visit in advance to see the facilities provided, how clean they are and where the dogs are kept. Talk to some of the employees and see how they treat the dogs—do they spend time with the dogs, play with them, exercise them, etc.? Also find out the kennel's policy on vaccinations and what they require. This is for all of the dogs' safety, since when dogs are kept together, there is a greater risk of diseases being passed from dog to dog.

IDENTIFICATION

Your Chow is your valued companion and friend. That is why you always keep a close eye on him and you have made sure that he cannot escape from the garden or wriggle out of his collar and run away from you. However, accidents can happen and there may come a time when your dog unexpectedly gets separated from you. If this unfortunate event should occur, the first thing on your mind will be finding him. Proper identification, including an ID tag, a tattoo, and possibly a microchip, will increase the chances of his being returned to you safely and quickly.

IDENTIFICATION

If your dog gets lost, he is not able to ask for directions home.

Identification tags fastened to the collar give important information—the dog's name, the owner's name, the owner's address and a telephone number where the owner can be reached. This makes it easy for whomever finds the dog to contact the owner and arrange to have the dog returned. An added advantage is that a person will be more likely to approach a lost dog who has ID tags on his collar; it tells the person that this is somebody's pet rather than a stray. This is the easiest and fastest method of identification provided that the tags stay on the collar and the collar stays on the dog.

Your Chow should never be without his identification tags.

HOUSEBREAKING AND TRAINING YOUR CHOW CHOW

DID YOU KNOW?

Dogs are the most honourable animals in existence. They consider another species (humans) as their own. They interface with you. You are their leader. Puppies perceive children to be on their level; their actions around small children are different from their behaviour around their adult masters.

You have not selected the Chow Chow because the breed is easy to train. On the contrary, the Chow Chow's reputation for obedience is sketchy at best, horrible at worst. Not unlike his Nordic cousins, the Spitz breeds, huskies and lapphunds, the Chow Chow can be difficult to convince to obey you. Chows are not like spaniels who live to please you or like hounds who will sell their souls for a chunk of cheese. Chows have dignity, Chows have philosophies, Chows have brains (which they store in rather thick skulls!).

The owner's approach to training the Chow Chow, however, is no different than training the more responsive breeds—it just requires more persistence, patience and good humour. Many Chows have been trained to perform complicated obedience tasks and excel in many kinds of trials—obedience, agility and beyond. No trainer doubts the intelligence of the Chow, but many would prefer not to have their techniques put to the test by a pig-headed, lion-faced, canine demigod!

To train your Chow Chow, you may like to enrol in an obedience class, where you have the advantage of a professional. Teach the dog good manners as you learn how and why he behaves the way he does. Find out how to communicate with your dog and how to recognise and understand his communications

TRAINING TIP

Dogs will do anything for your attention. If you reward the dog when he is calm and resting, you will develop a well-mannered dog. If, on the other hand, you greet your dog excitedly and encourage him to wrestle and roughhouse with you, the dog will greet you the same way and you will have a hyper dog on your hands.

with you. Suddenly the dog takes on a new role in your life—he is clever, interesting, well-behaved and fun to be with. He demonstrates his bond of devotion to you daily. In other words, your Chow Chow does wonders for your ego because he constantly reminds you that you are not only his leader, you are his hero!

Those involved with teaching dog obedience and counselling owners about their dogs' behaviour have discovered some interesting facts about dog ownership. For example, training dogs when they are puppies results in the highest rate of success in developing well-mannered and well-adjusted adult dogs. Training an older dog, from six

TRAINING TIP

Training a dog is a life experience. Many parents admit that much of what they know about raising children they learned from caring for their dogs. Dogs respond to love, fairness and guidance, just as children do. Become a good dog owner and you may become an even better parent.

Chows are challenging dogs to train. Of course they are trainable, but one has to take the breed's unique personality into account when considering the approach to training.

DID YOU KNOW?

To a dog's way of thinking, your hands are like his mouth in terms of a defence mechanism. If you squeeze him too tightly, he might

just bite you because that would be his normal response. This is not aggressive biting and, although all biting should be discouraged, you need the discipline in learning how to handle your dog.

months to six years of age, can produce almost equal results provided that the owner accepts the dog's slower rate of learning capability and is willing to work patiently to help the dog succeed at developing to his fullest potential. Unfortunately, many owners of untrained adult dogs lack the patience factor, so they do not persist until their dogs are successful at learning particular behaviours.

Training a puppy aged 10 to 16 weeks (20 weeks at the most)

MEALTIME

Mealtime should be a peaceful time for your Chow. Do not put his food and water bowls in a high-traffic area in the house. For example, give him his own little corner of the kitchen

where he can eat undisturbed and where he will not be underfoot. Do not allow small children or other family members to disturb the dog when he is eating.

is like working with a dry sponge in a pool of water. The pup soaks up whatever you show him and constantly looks for more things to do and learn. At this early age, his body is not yet producing hormones, and therein lies the reason for such a high rate of success. Without hormones, he is focused on his owners and not particularly interested in investigating other places, dogs, people, etc. You are his leader: his provider of food, water, shelter and security. He latches onto you and wants to stay close. He will usually follow you from room to room, will not let you out of his sight when you are outdoors with him, and will respond in like manner to the people and animals you encounter. If you greet a friend warmly, he will be happy to greet the person as well. If, however, you are hesitant, even anxious, about the approach of a stranger, he will respond accordingly.

Once the puppy begins to produce hormones, his natural curiosity emerges and he begins to investigate the world around him. It is at this time when you may notice that the untrained dog begins to wander away from you and even ignore your commands to stay close. When this behaviour becomes a problem, the owner has two choices: get rid of the dog or

TRAINING TIP

If you start with a normal, healthy dog and give him time, patience and some carefully executed lessons, you will reap the rewards of that training for

the life of the dog. And what a life it will be! The two of you will find immeasurable pleasure in the companionship you have built together with love, respect and understanding.

THINK BEFORE YOU BARK!

Dogs are sensitive to their master's moods and emotions. Use your voice wisely when communicating with your dog. Never raise your voice at your dog unless you are angry and trying to correct him. 'Barking' at your dog can become as meaningless as 'dogspeak' is to you. Think before you bark!

train him. It is strongly urged that you choose the latter option.

There are usually classes within a reasonable distance from the owner's home, but you can also do a lot to train your dog yourself. Sometimes there are classes available but the tuition is too costly. Whatever the circumstances, the solution to the problem of lack of lesson availability lies within the pages of this book.

This chapter is devoted to helping you train your Chow Chow at home. If the recommended procedures are followed faithfully, you may expect positive results that will prove rewarding both to you and your dog.

Whether your new charge is a puppy or a mature adult, the methods of teaching and the techniques we use in training basic behaviours are the same. After all, no dog, whether puppy or adult, likes harsh or inhumane methods. All creatures, however, respond favourably to gentle motivational methods and sincere praise and encouragement. Now let us get started.

HOUSEBREAKING

You can train a puppy to relieve itself wherever you choose, but it must be somewhere suitable. You should bear in mind from the outset that when your puppy is old enough to go out in public places, any canine deposits must be removed at once. You will always have to carry with you a small plastic bag or 'poop-scoop.'

Outdoor training includes such surfaces as grass, soil or earth and cement. Indoor training usually means training your dog to newspaper.

CANINE DEVELOPMENT SCHEDULE

It is important to understand how and at what age a puppy develops into adulthood. If you are a puppy owner, consult the following Canine Development Schedule to determine the stage of development your puppy is currently experiencing. This knowledge will help you as you work with the puppy in the weeks and months ahead.

Period	Age	Characteristics
First to Third	Birth to Seven Weeks	Puppy needs food, sleep and warmth, and responds to simple and gentle touching. Needs mother for security and disciplining. Needs littermates for learning and interacting with other dogs. Pup learns to function within a pack and learns pack order of dominance. Begin socialising with adults and children for short periods. Begins to become aware of its environment.
Fourth	Eight to Twelve Weeks	Brain is fully developed. Needs socialising with outside world. Remove from mother and littermates. Needs to change from canine pack to human pack. Human dominance necessary. Fear period occurs between 8 and 16 weeks. Avoid fright and pain.
Fifth	Thirteen to Sixteen Weeks	Training and formal obedience should begin. Less association with other dogs, more with people, places, situations. Period will pass easily if you remember this is pup's change-to-adolescence time. Be firm and fair. Flight instinct prominent. Permissiveness and over-disciplining can do permanent damage. Praise for good behaviour.
Juvenile	Four to Eight Months	Another fear period about 7 to 8 months of age. It passes quickly, but be cautious of fright and pain. Sexual maturity reached. Dominant traits established. Dog should understand sit, down, come and stay by now.

Note: These are approximate time frames. Allow for individual differences in puppies.

HOUSEBREAKING TIP

Never line your pup's sleeping area with newspaper. Puppy litters are usually raised on newspaper and, once in your home, the puppy will immediately associate newspaper with voiding. Never put

newspaper on any floor while housetraining, as this will only confuse the puppy. If you are paper-training him, use paper in his designated relief area ONLY. Finally, restrict water intake after evening meals. Offer a few licks at a time—never let a young puppy gulp water after meals.

When deciding on the surface and location that you will want your Chow Chow to use, be sure it is going to be permanent. Training your dog to grass and then changing your mind two months later is extremely difficult for both dog and owner.

Next, choose the command you will use each and every time you want your puppy to void. 'Be quick' and 'Hurry up' are examples of commands commonly used by dog owners.

Get in the habit of giving the puppy your chosen relief command before you take him out. That way, when he becomes an adult, you will be able to determine if he wants to go out when you ask him. A confirmation will be signs of interest, wagging his tail, watching you intently, going to the door, etc.

PUPPY'S NEEDS

Puppy needs to relieve himself after play periods, after each meal, after he has been sleeping and any time he indicates that he is looking for a place to urinate or defecate.

The urinary and intestinal tract muscles of very young puppies are not fully developed. Therefore, like human babies, puppies need to relieve themselves frequently.

Take your puppy out often—every hour for an eight-week-old, for example, and always immediately after sleeping and eating. The older the puppy, the less often he will need to relieve himself. Finally, as a mature healthy adult, he will require only three to five relief trips per day.

HOUSING

Since the types of housing and control you provide for your puppy have a direct relationship on the success of housetraining, we consider the various aspects of both before we begin training.

Bringing a new puppy home and turning him loose in your house can be compared to turning a child loose in a sports arena and telling the child that the place is all his! The sheer enormity of the place would be too much for him to handle.

Instead, offer the puppy clearly defined areas where he can play, sleep, eat and live. A room of the house where the family gathers is the most obvious choice. Puppies are social animals and need to feel a part of the pack right from the start. Hearing your voice, watching you while you are doing things and smelling you nearby are all positive reinforcers that he is now a member of your pack. Usually a family room, the kitchen or a nearby adjoining breakfast area is ideal for providing safety and security for both puppy and owner.

Within that room there should be a smaller area which the puppy can call his own. An alcove, a wire or fibreglass dog crate or a fenced (not boarded!) corner from which he can view the activities of his new family will be fine. The size of the area or crate is the key factor here. The area must be large enough for the puppy to lie down and stretch out as well as stand up without rubbing his head on the top, yet small enough so that he cannot relieve himself at one end and sleep at the other without coming into contact with his droppings until fully trained to relieve himself outside.

Dogs are, by nature, clean animals and will not remain close to their relief areas unless forced to do so. In those cases, they then become dirty dogs

TRAINING TIP

Your dog is actually training you at the same time you are training him. Dogs do things to get attention.

They usually repeat whatever succeeds in getting your attention.

The crate has to be your Chow's home within a home. Crates have many useful functions and can be used both indoors and out.

and usually remain that way for life.

The designated area should be lined with clean bedding and a toy. Water must always be available, in a non-spill container.

Control

By control, we mean helping the puppy to create a lifestyle pattern that will be compatible to that of his human pack (YOU!). Just as we guide little children to learn our way of life, we must show the puppy when it is time to play, eat, sleep, exercise and even entertain himself.

Your puppy should always sleep in his crate. He should also learn that, during times of household confusion and excessive human activity such as at breakfast when family members are preparing for the day, he can play by himself in relative safety and comfort in his designated area. Each time you leave the puppy alone, he should understand exactly where he is to stay. Puppies are chewers. They cannot tell the difference between lamp cords, television wires, shoes, table legs, etc. Chewing into a television wire, for example, can be fatal to the puppy while a shorted wire can start a fire in the house.

If the puppy chews on the arm of the chair when he is alone, you will probably discipline him angrily when you get home. Thus, he makes the association that your coming home means he is going to be punished. (He will not remember chewing the chair and is incapable of making the

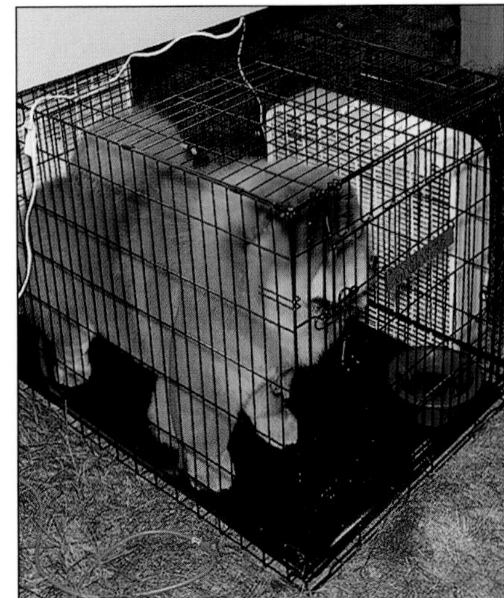
A wire crate is preferred for outdoor use, as it allows air to flow through freely. The crate pictured is a good size for the Chow; it should be no smaller.

association of the discipline with his naughty deed.)

Other times of excitement, such as family parties, etc., can be fun for the puppy providing he can view the activities from the security of his designated area. He is not underfoot and he is not being fed all sorts of titbits that will probably cause him stomach distress, yet he still feels a part of the fun.

SCHEDULE

A puppy should be taken to his relief area each time he is released from his designated area, after meals, after a play session and when he first awakens in the morning (at age eight weeks, this can mean 5 a.m.!). The puppy will indicate that he's ready 'to go' by circling or sniffing busily—-do not misinterpret these signs. For a puppy less than ten weeks of age, a routine of taking him out every hour is necessary. As the

THE GOLDEN RULE

The golden rule of dog training is simple. For each 'question' (command), there is only one correct answer (reaction). One command = one reaction. Keep practising the command until the dog reacts correctly without hesitating. Be repetitive but not monotonous. Dogs get bored just as people do!

PRACTICE MAKES PERFECT!

- Have training lessons with your dog every day in several short segments—three to five times a day for a few minutes at a time is ideal.
- Do not have long practice sessions. The dog will become easily bored.
- Never practise when you are tired, ill, worried or in an otherwise negative mood. This will transmit to the dog and may have an adverse effect on its performance.

Think fun, short and above all POSITIVE! End each session on a high note, rather than a failed exercise, and make sure to give a lot of praise. Enjoy the training and help your dog enjoy it, too.

HOW MANY TIMES A DAY?

AGE	RELIEF TRIPS
To 14 weeks	10
14–22 weeks	8
22–32 weeks	6
Adulthood (dog stops growing)	4

These are estimates, of course, but they are a guide to the MINIMUM opportunities a dog should have each day to relieve itself.

puppy grows, he will be able to wait for longer periods of time.

Keep trips to his relief area short. Stay no more than five or six minutes and then return to the house. If he goes during that time, praise him lavishly and take him indoors immediately. If he does not, but he has an accident when you go back indoors, pick him up immediately, say 'No! No!' and return to his relief area. Wait a few minutes, then return to the house again. Never hit a puppy or rub his face in urine or excrement when he has had an accident!

Once indoors, put the puppy in his crate until you have had time to clean up his accident. Then release him to the family area and watch him more closely than before. Chances are, his accident was a result of your not picking up his signal or waiting too long before offering him the opportunity to relieve himself. Never hold a grudge against the puppy for accidents.

Let the puppy learn that going outdoors means it is time to relieve himself, not play. Once trained, he will be able to play indoors and out and still differentiate between the times for play versus the times for relief.

Help him develop regular hours for naps, being alone, playing by himself and just resting, all in his crate. Encourage him to entertain himself while you are busy with your activities. Let him learn that having you near is comforting, but it is not your main purpose in life to provide him with undivided attention.

Each time you put a puppy in his own area, use the same command, whatever suits best. Soon he will run to his crate or special area when he hears you say those words.

Crate training provides safety for you, the puppy and the home. It also provides the puppy with a feeling of security, and that helps the puppy achieve self-confidence and clean habits.

Remember that one of the primary ingredients in housetraining your puppy is control. Regardless of your

TRAINING TIP

Stand up straight and authoritatively when giving your dog commands. Do not issue commands when lying on the floor or lying on your back on the sofa.

If you are on your hands and knees when you give a command, your dog will think you are positioning yourself to play.

HOUSEBREAKING TIP

Do not carry your dog to his toilet area. Lead him there on a leash or, better yet, encourage him to follow you to the spot. If you start carrying him to his spot, you might end up

doing this routine forever and your dog will have the satisfaction of having trained YOU.

lifestyle, there will always be occasions when you will need to have a place where your dog can stay and be happy and safe. Crate training is the answer for now and in the future.

In conclusion, a few key elements are really all you need for a successful house training method—consistency, frequency, praise, control and supervision. By following these procedures with a normal, healthy puppy, you and the puppy will soon be past the stage of 'accidents' and ready to move on to a full and rewarding life together.

THE SUCCESS METHOD

Success that comes by luck is usually short lived. Success that comes by well-thought-out proven methods is often more easily achieved and permanent. This is the Success Method. It is designed to give you, the puppy owner, a simple yet proven way to help your puppy develop clean living habits and a feeling of security in his new environment.

THE SUCCESS METHOD

1 Tell the puppy 'Crate time!' and place him in the crate with a small treat (a piece of cheese or half of a biscuit). Let him stay in the crate for five minutes while you are in the same room. Then release him and praise lavishly. Never release him when he is fussing. Wait until he is quiet before you let him out.

2 Repeat Step 1 several times a day.

3 The next day, place the puppy in the crate as before. Let him stay there for ten minutes. Do this several times.

4 Continue building time in five-minute increments until the puppy stays in his crate for 30 minutes with you in the room. Always take him to his relief area after prolonged periods in his crate.

5 Now go back to Step 1 and let the puppy stay in his crate for five minutes, this time while you are out of the room.

6 Once again, build crate time in five-minute increments with you out of the room. When the puppy will stay willingly in his crate (he may even fall asleep!) for 30 minutes with you out of the room, he will be ready to stay in it for several hours at a time.

6 Steps to Successful Crate Training

ROLES OF DISCIPLINE, REWARD AND PUNISHMENT

Discipline, training one to act in accordance with rules, brings order to life. It is as simple as that. Without discipline, particularly in a group society, chaos reigns supreme and the group will eventually perish. Humans and canines are social animals and need some form of discipline in order to function effectively. They must procure food, protect their home base and their young and reproduce to keep the species going.

If there were no discipline in the lives of social animals, they would eventually die from starvation and/or predation by other stronger animals.

In the case of domestic canines, dogs need discipline in their lives in order to understand how their pack (you and other family members) functions and how they must act in order to survive.

HOUSEBREAKING TIP

By providing sleeping and resting quarters that fit the dog, and offering frequent opportunities to relieve himself outside his quarters, the puppy quickly learns that the outdoors (or the newspaper if you are training him to paper) is the place to go when he needs to urinate or defecate. It also reinforces his innate desire to keep his sleeping quarters clean. This, in turn, helps develop the muscle control that will eventually produce a dog with clean living habits.

You simply must clean up after your dog. Pet shops have handy gadgets to make the task simpler.

A large humane society in a highly populated area recently surveyed dog owners regarding their satisfaction with their relationships with their dogs. People who had trained their dogs were 75% more satisfied with their pets than those who had never trained their dogs.

Dr Edward Thorndike, a psychologist, established *Thorndike's Theory of Learning*, which states that a behaviour that results in a pleasant event tends to be repeated. A behaviour that results in an unpleasant event tends not to be repeated. It is this theory on which training methods are based today. For example, if you manipulate a dog to perform a specific behaviour and reward him for doing it, he is likely to do it again because he enjoyed the end result.

Occasionally, punishment, a penalty inflicted for an offence, is necessary. The best type of

INFORMATION . . .

The puppy should also have regular play and exercise sessions when he is with you or a family member. Exercise for a very young puppy can consist of a

short walk around the house or garden. Playing can include fetching games with a large ball or a special raggy. (All puppies teethe and need soft things upon which to chew.) Remember to restrict play periods to indoors within his living area (the family room, for example) until he is completely housetrained.

punishment often comes from an outside source. For example, a child is told not to touch the stove because he may get burned. He disobeys and touches the stove. In doing so, he receives a burn. From that time on, he respects the heat of the stove and avoids contact with it. Therefore, a behaviour that results in an unpleasant event tends not to be repeated.

A good example of a dog learning the hard way is the dog who chases the house cat. He is told many times to leave the cat alone, yet he persists in teasing the cat. Then, one day he begins chasing the cat but the cat turns and swipes a claw across the dog's face, leaving him with a painful gash on his nose. The final result is that the dog stops chasing the cat.

TRAINING EQUIPMENT

Collar and Lead

For a Chow Chow the collar and lead that you use for training must be one with which you are easily able to work, not too heavy for the dog and perfectly safe.

Treats

Have a bag of treats on hand. Something nutritious and easy to swallow works best. Use a soft treat, a chunk of cheese or a piece of cooked chicken rather than a dry biscuit. By the time the dog has finished chewing a dry treat, he will forget why he is being rewarded in the first place! Using food rewards will not teach a dog to beg at the table—the only way to teach a dog to beg at the table is to give him food from the table. In

DID YOU KNOW?

Dogs are as different from each other as people are. What works for one dog may not work for another. Have an open mind. If one method of training is unsuccessful, try another.

training, rewarding the dog with a food treat will help him associate praise and the treats with learning new behaviours that obviously please his owner.

TRAINING BEGINS: ASK THE DOG A QUESTION

In order to teach your dog anything, you must first get his attention. After all, he cannot learn anything if he is looking away from you with his mind on something else.

To get his attention, ask him, 'School?' and immediately walk over to him and give him a treat as you tell him 'Good dog.' Wait a minute or two and repeat the routine, this time with a treat in your hand as you approach within a foot of the dog. Do not go directly to him, but stop about a foot short of him and hold out the treat as you ask, 'School?' He will see you approaching with a treat in your hand and most likely begin walking toward you. As you meet, give him the treat and praise again.

The third time, ask the question, have a treat in your hand and walk only a short distance toward the dog so that he must walk almost all the way to you. As he reaches you, give him the treat and praise again.

By this time, the dog will probably be getting the idea that if he pays attention to you,

TRAINING TIP

Dogs do not understand our language. They can be trained to react to a certain sound, at a certain volume. If you say 'No, Oliver' in a very soft pleasant voice it will not have the same meaning as 'No, Oliver!' when you shout it as loud as you can. You should never use the dog's name during a reprimand, just the command NO! Since dogs don't understand words, comics often use dogs trained with opposite meanings. Thus, when the comic commands his dog to SIT the dog will stand up, and vice versa.

It's hard to distract any dog when he's found something to investigate, but your Chow should learn to always respond to the sound of your voice and to give you his attention.

> **DID YOU KNOW?**
>
> If you want to be successful in training your dog, you have four rules to obey yourself:
> 1. Develop an understanding of how a dog thinks.
> 2. Do not blame the dog for lack of communication.
> 3. Define your dog's personality and act accordingly.
> 4. Have patience and be consistent.

especially when you ask that question, it will pay off in treats and enjoyable activities for him. In other words, he learns that 'school' means doing enjoyable things with you that result in treats and positive attention for him.

Remember that the dog does not understand your verbal language; he only recognises sounds. Your question translates to a series of sounds for him,

and those sounds become the signal to go to you and pay attention; if he does, he will get to interact with you plus receive treats and praise.

THE BASIC COMMANDS

TEACHING SIT

Now that you have the dog's attention, attach his lead and hold it in your left hand and a food treat in your right. Place your food hand at the dog's nose and let him lick the treat but not take it from you. Say 'Sit' and slowly raise your food hand from in front of the dog's nose up over his head so that he is looking at the ceiling. As he bends his head upward, he will have to bend his knees to maintain his balance. As he bends his knees, he will assume a sit position. At that point, release the food treat and praise lavishly with comments such as 'Good dog! Good sit!,' etc. Remember to always praise enthusiastically, because dogs relish verbal praise from their owners and feel so proud of themselves whenever they accomplish a behaviour.

You will not use food forever in getting the dog to obey your commands. Food is only used to teach new behaviours, and once the dog knows what you want when you give a specific command, you will wean him off the food treats but still maintain the verbal praise. After all, you will always have your voice with you, and there will be many times when you have no food rewards but expect the dog to obey.

TEACHING DOWN

Teaching the down exercise is easy when you understand how the dog perceives the down position, and it is very difficult when you do not. Dogs perceive the down position as a submissive one; therefore, teaching the down exercise using a forceful method can sometimes make the dog develop such a fear of the down that he either runs away when you say 'Down' or he attempts to snap at the person who tries to force him down.

Have the dog sit close alongside your left leg, facing in the same direction as you are. Hold the lead in your left hand and a food treat in your right. Now place your left hand lightly on the top of the dog's shoulders where they meet above the spinal cord. Do not push down on the dog's shoulders; simply rest your left hand there so you can guide the dog to lie down close to your left leg rather than to swing away from your side when he drops.

> **TRAINING TIP**
>
> A dog in jeopardy never lies down. He stays alert on his feet because instinct tells him that he may have to run away or fight for his survival. Therefore, if a dog feels threatened or anxious, he will not lie down. Consequently, it is important to have the dog calm and relaxed as he learns the down exercise.

Now place the food hand at the dog's nose, say 'Down' very softly (almost a whisper), and slowly lower the food hand to the dog's front feet. When the food hand reaches the floor, begin moving it forward along the floor in front of the dog. Keep talking softly to the dog, saying things like, 'Do you want this treat? You can do this, good dog.' Your reassuring tone of voice will help calm the dog as he tries to follow the food hand in order to get the treat.

When the dog's elbows touch the floor, release the food and praise softly. Try to get the dog to maintain that down position for several seconds before you let him sit up again. The goal here is to get the dog to settle down and not feel threatened in the down position.

Teaching Stay

It is easy to teach the dog to stay in either a sit or a down position. Again, we use food and praise during the teaching process as we help the dog to understand exactly what it is that we are expecting him to do.

To teach the sit/stay, start with the dog sitting on your left side as before and hold the lead in your left hand. Have a food treat in your right hand and place your food hand at the dog's nose. Say 'Stay' and step out on your right foot to stand directly in front of the dog, toe to toe, as he licks and nibbles the treat. Be sure to keep his head facing upward to maintain the sit position. Count to five and then swing around to stand next to the dog again with him on your left. As soon as you get back to the original position, release the food and praise lavishly.

To teach the down/stay, do the down as previously described. As soon as the dog lies down, say 'Stay' and step out on your right foot just as you did in the sit/stay. Count to five and then return to stand beside the dog with him on your left side. Release the treat and praise as always.

Within a week or ten days, you can begin to add a bit of distance between you and your dog when you leave him. When you do, use your left hand open with the palm facing the dog as a stay signal, much the same as the hand signal a police officer uses to stop traffic at an intersection. Hold the food treat in your right hand as before, but this time the food is not touching the dog's nose. He will watch the food hand and quickly learn that he is going to get that treat as soon as you return to his side.

When you can stand 1 metre away from your dog for 30 seconds, you can then begin building time and distance in both stays. Eventually, the dog can be expected to remain in the stay position for prolonged periods of time until you return to him or call him to you. Always praise lavishly when he stays.

Once your dog has learned to sit, you can teach him the sit/stay rather easily. Of course, it doesn't hurt to use a treat for extra motivation!

Teaching Come

If you make teaching 'come' an enjoyable experience, you should never have a 'student' that does not love the game or that fails to come when called. The secret, it seems, is never to teach the word 'come.'

At times when an owner most wants his dog to come when called, the owner is likely upset or anxious and he allows these feelings to come through in the tone of his voice when he calls his dog. Hearing that desperation in his owner's voice, the dog fears the results of going to him and therefore either disobeys outright or runs in the opposite direction. The

TRAINING TIP

Never call your dog to come to you for a correction or scold him when he reaches you. That is the quickest way to turn a 'Come' command into 'Go away fast!' Dogs think only in the present tense, and your dog will connect the scolding with coming to you, not with the misbehaviour of a few moments earlier.

If your Chow learns as a pup to associate coming to you with treats and praise, he will think of it as a positive experience and should never fail to come when called.

secret, therefore, is to teach the dog a game and, when you want him to come to you, simply play the game. It is practically a no-fail solution!

To begin, have several members of your family take a few food treats and each go into a different room in the house. Take turns calling the dog, and each person should celebrate the dog's finding him with a treat and lots of happy praise. When a person calls the dog, he is actually inviting the dog to find him and get a treat as a reward for 'winning.'

A few turns of the 'Where are you?' game and the dog will understand that everyone is playing the game and that each person has a big celebration awaiting his success at locating them. Once he learns to love the game, simply calling out 'Where are you?' will bring him running from wherever he is when he hears that all-important question.

The come command is

CONSISTENCY PAYS OFF

Dogs need consistency in their feeding schedule, exercise and toilet breaks and in the verbal commands you use. If you use 'Stay' on Monday and 'Stay here, please' on Tuesday, you will confuse your dog. Don't demand perfect behaviour during training classes and then let him have the run of the house the rest of the day. Above all, lavish praise on your pet consistently every time he does something right. The more he feels he is pleasing you, the more willing he will be to learn.

recognised as one of the most important things to teach a dog, but there are trainers who work with thousands of dogs and never teach the actual word 'Come.' Yet these dogs will race to respond to a person who uses the dog's name followed by 'Where are you?' For example, a woman has a 12-year-old companion dog who went blind, but who never fails to locate her owner when asked, 'Where are you?'

Children, in particular, love to play this game with their dogs. Children can hide in smaller places like a shower or bath, behind a bed or under a table. The dog needs to work a little bit harder to find these hiding places, but when he does he loves to celebrate with a treat and a tussle with a favourite youngster.

Teaching Heel

Heeling means that the dog walks beside the owner without pulling. It takes time and patience on the owner's part to succeed at teaching the dog that he (the owner) will not proceed unless the dog is walking calmly beside him. Pulling out ahead on the lead is definitely not acceptable.

Begin by holding the lead in your left hand as the dog sits beside your left leg. Move the loop end of the lead to your

TRAINING TIP

When calling the dog, do not say 'Come.' Say things like, 'Rover, where are you? See if you can find me! I have a biscuit for you!' Keep up a constant line of chatter with coaxing sounds

and frequent questions such as, 'Where are you?' The dog will learn to follow the sound of your voice to locate you and receive his reward.

HOW TO WEAN THE 'TREAT HOG'

If you have trained your dog by rewarding him with a treat each time he performs a command, he may soon decide that without the treat, he won't sit, stay or come. The best way to fix this problem is to start asking your dog

to do certain commands twice before being rewarded. Slowly increase the number of commands given and then vary the number: three sits and a treat one day, five sits for a biscuit the next day. Your dog will soon realise that there is no set number of sits before he gets his reward, and he'll likely do it the first time you ask in the hope of being rewarded sooner rather than later.

right hand but keep your left hand short on the lead so it keeps the dog in close next to you.

Say 'Heel' and step forward on your left foot. Keep the dog close to you and take three steps. Stop and have the dog sit next to you in what we now call the 'heel position.' Praise verbally, but do not touch the dog. Hesitate a moment and begin again with 'Heel,' taking three steps and stopping, at which point the dog is told to sit again.

Your goal here is to have the dog walk those three steps without pulling on the lead. When he will walk calmly beside you for three steps without pulling, increase the number of steps you take to five. When he will walk politely beside you while you take five steps, you can increase the length of your walk to ten steps. Keep increasing the length of your stroll until the dog will walk quietly beside you without pulling as long as you want him to heel. When you stop heeling, indicate to the dog that the exercise is over by verbally praising as you pet him and say 'OK, good dog.' The 'OK' is used as a release word meaning that the exercise is finished and the dog is free to relax.

If you are dealing with a dog who insists on pulling you

around, simply 'put on your brakes' and stand your ground until the dog realises that the two of you are not going anywhere until he is beside you and moving at your pace, not his. It may take some time just standing there to convince the dog that you are the leader and you will be the one to decide on the direction and speed of your travel.

Each time the dog looks up at you or slows down to give a slack lead between the two of you, quietly praise him and say, 'Good heel. Good dog.' Eventually, the dog will begin to respond and within a few days he will be walking politely beside you without pulling on the lead. At first, the training sessions should be kept short and very positive; soon the dog will be able to walk nicely with you for increasingly longer distances. Remember also to give the dog free time and the opportunity to run and play when you have finished heel practice.

TRAINING TIP

If you are walking your dog and he suddenly stops and looks straight into your eyes, ignore him. Pull the leash and lead him into the direction you want to walk.

TRAINING TIP

If you begin teaching the heel by taking long walks and letting the dog pull you along, he misinterprets this action as an acceptable form of taking a walk.

When you pull back on the lead to counteract his pulling, he reads that tug as a signal to pull even harder!

WEANING OFF FOOD IN TRAINING

Food is used in training new behaviours. Once the dog understands what behaviour goes with a specific command, it is time to start weaning him off the food treats. At first, give a treat after each exercise. Then, start to give a treat only after every other exercise. Mix up the times when you offer a food reward and the times when you only offer praise so that the dog will never know

FEAR AGGRESSION

Pups who are subjected to physical abuse during training commonly end up with behavioural problems as adults. One common result of abuse is fear aggression, in which a dog will lash out, bare his teeth, snarl and finally bite someone by whom he feels threatened. For example, your daughter may be playing with the dog one afternoon. As they play hide-and-seek, she backs the dog into a corner, and as she attempts to tease him playfully, he bites her hand. Examine the cause of this behaviour. Did your daughter ever hit the dog? Did someone who resembles your daughter hit or scream at the dog? Fortunately, fear aggression is relatively easy to correct. Have your daughter engage in only positive activities with the dog, such as feeding, petting and walking. She should not give any corrections or negative feedback. If the dog still growls or cowers away from her, allow someone else to accompany them. After approximately one week, the dog should feel that he can rely on her for many positive things, and he will also be prevented from reacting fearfully towards anyone who might resemble her.

when he is going to receive both food and praise and when he is going to receive only praise. This is called a variable ratio reward system and it proves successful because there is always the chance that the owner will produce a treat, so the dog never stops trying for that reward. No matter what, ALWAYS give verbal praise.

OBEDIENCE CLASSES

It is a good idea to enrol in an obedience class if one is available in your area. If yours is a show dog, ringcraft classes would be more appropriate. Many areas have dog clubs that offer basic obedience training as well as preparatory

DID YOU KNOW?

Occasionally, a dog and owner who have not attended formal classes have been able to earn entry-level titles by obtaining competition rules and regulations from a local kennel club and practising on their own to a degree of perfection. Obtaining the higher level titles, however, almost always requires extensive training under the tutelage of experienced instructors. In addition, the more difficult levels require more specialised equipment whereas the lower levels do not.

classes for obedience competition. There are also local dog trainers who offer similar classes.

At obedience trials, dogs can earn titles at various levels of competition. The beginning levels of competition include basic behaviours such as sit, down, heel, etc. The more advanced levels of competition include jumping, retrieving, scent discrimination and signal work. The advanced levels require a dog and owner to put a lot of time and effort into their training and the titles that can be earned at these levels of competition are very prestigious.

OTHER ACTIVITIES FOR LIFE

Whether a dog is trained in the structured environment of a class or alone with his owner at home, there are many activities that can bring fun and rewards to both owner and dog once they have mastered basic control.

Teaching the dog to help out around the home, in the garden or on the farm provides great satisfaction to both dog and owner. In addition, the dog's help makes life a little easier for his owner and raises his stature as a valued companion to his family. It helps give the dog a purpose by occupying his mind and providing an outlet for his energy.

If you are interested in participating in organised competition with your Chow Chow, there are activities other than obedience in which you and your dog can become involved. Agility is a popular and enjoyable sport where dogs run through an obstacle course that includes various jumps, tunnels and other exercises to test the dog's speed and coordination. The owners run beside their dogs to give commands and to guide them through the course. Although competitive, the focus is on fun—it's fun to do, fun to watch, and great exercise.

DID YOU KNOW?

Your dog may not be the next Lassie, but every pet has the potential to do some tricks well. Identify his natural talents and hone them. Is your dog always happy and upbeat? Teach him to wag his tail or give you his paw on command. Real homebodies can be trained to do household chores, such as carrying dirty washing or retrieving the morning paper.

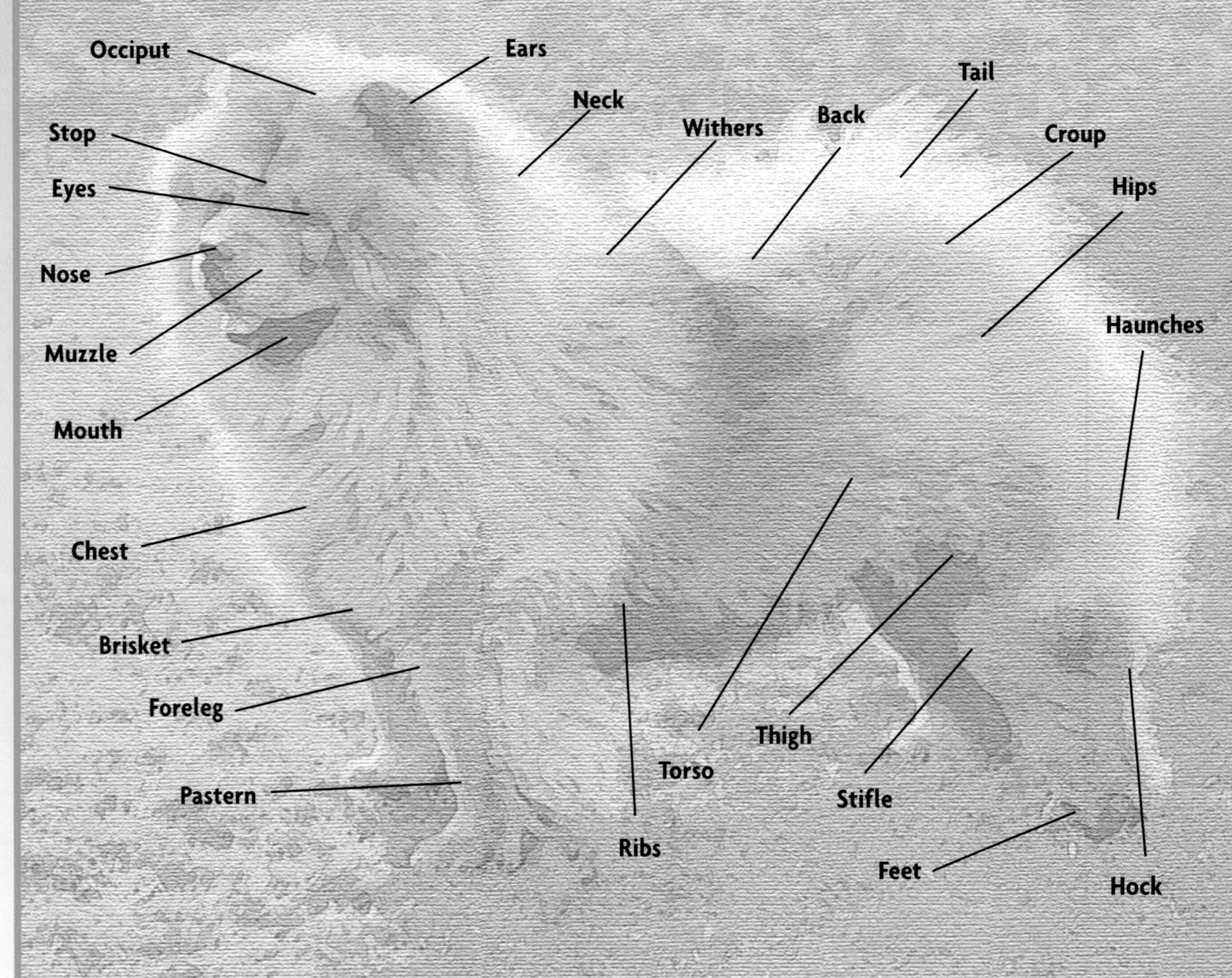

Physical Structure of the Chow Chow

HEALTH CARE OF YOUR CHOW CHOW

Dogs suffer many of the same physical illnesses as people. They might even share many of the same psychological problems. Since people usually know more about human diseases than canine maladies, many of the terms used in this chapter will be familiar but not necessarily those used by veterinary surgeons. We will use the term *x-ray*, instead of the more acceptable term *radiograph*. We will also use the familiar term *symptoms* even though dogs don't have symptoms, which are verbal descriptions of the patient's feelings; dogs have *clinical signs*. Since dogs can't speak, we have to look for clinical signs...but we still use the term symptoms in this book.

As a general rule, medicine is practised. That term is not arbitrary. Medicine is a constantly changing art as we learn more and more about genetics, electronic aids (like CAT scans) and daily laboratory advances. There are many dog maladies, like canine hip dysplasia, which are not universally treated in the same manner. Some veterinary surgeons opt for surgery more often than others do.

SELECTING A VETERINARY SURGEON

Your selection of a veterinary surgeon should not be based upon personality (as most are) but upon their convenience to your home. You require a veterinary surgeon who is close because you might have emergencies or need to make multiple visits for treatments. You require a vet who has services that you might require such as tattooing and grooming, as well as sophisticated pet supplies and a good reputation for ability and responsiveness. There is nothing

One of the first things you should do with your Chow puppy is to bring him to your local veterinary surgeon and have him examined for health problems.

Internal Organs of the Chow Chow

more frustrating than having to wait a day or more to get a response from your veterinary surgeon.

All veterinary surgeons are licensed and their diplomas and/or certificates should be displayed in their waiting rooms. There are, however, many veterinary specialities that usually require further studies and internships. There are specialists in heart problems (veterinary cardiologists), skin problems (veterinary dermatologists), teeth and gum problems (veterinary dentists), eye problems (veterinary ophthalmologists) and x-rays (veterinary radiologists), and surgeons who have specialities in bones, muscles or other organs. Most veterinary surgeons do routine surgery such as neutering, stitching up wounds and docking tails for those breeds in which such is required for show purposes. When the problem affecting your dog is serious, it is not unusual or impudent to get another medical opinion, although in Britain you are obliged to advise the vets concerned about this. You might also want to compare costs amongst several veterinary surgeons. Sophisticated health care and veterinary services can be very costly. Important decisions are often based upon financial considerations.

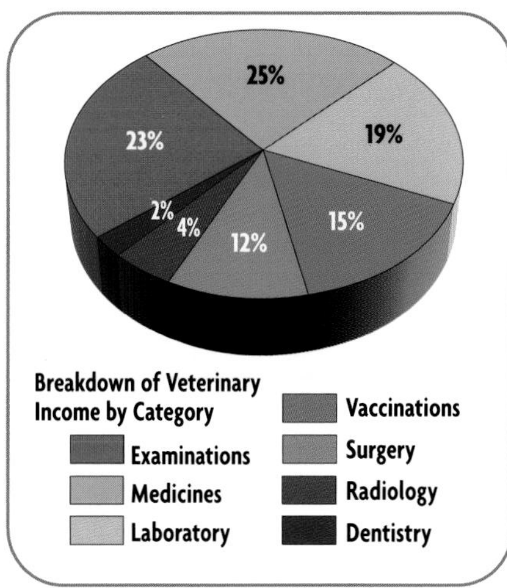

A typical American vet's income, categorised according to services provided. This survey dealt with small-animal practices.

DID YOU KNOW?

Male dogs are neutered. The operation removes the testicles and requires that the dog be anaesthetised. Recovery takes about one week. Females are spayed. This is major surgery and it usually takes a bitch two weeks to recover.

PREVENTATIVE MEDICINE

It is much easier, less costly and more effective to practise preventative medicine than to fight bouts of illness and disease. Properly bred puppies come from parents that were selected based upon their genetic disease profile. Their mothers should have been vaccinated, free of all internal and external parasites, and properly nourished. For these reasons, a visit to the veterinary surgeon who cared for the dam is recommended. The dam can pass

Skeletal Structure of the Chow Chow

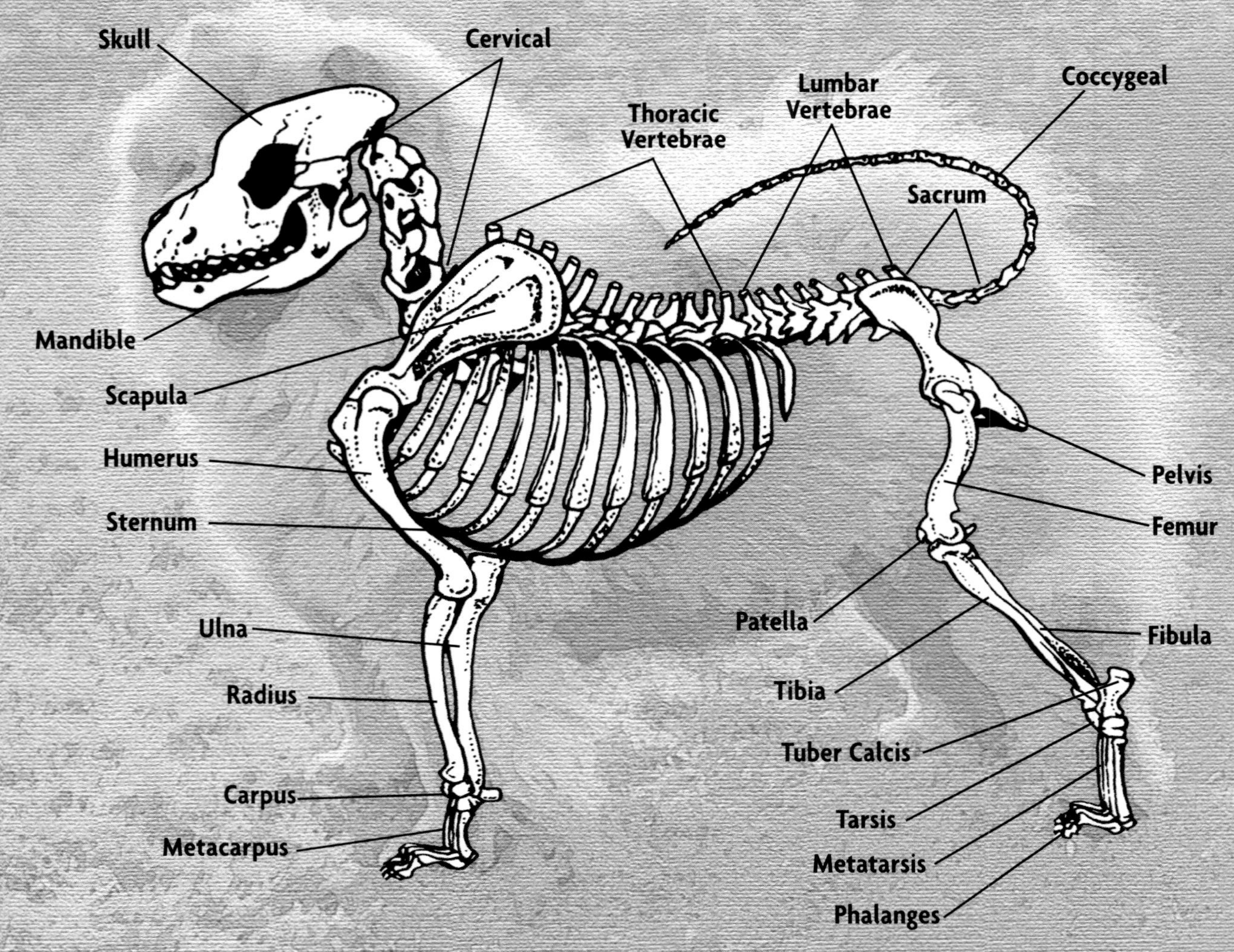

on disease resistance to her puppies, which can last for eight to ten weeks. She can also pass on parasites and many infections. That's why you should visit the veterinary surgeon who cared for the dam.

Vaccination Scheduling

Most vaccinations are given by injection and should only be done by a veterinary surgeon. Both he and you should keep a record of the date of the injection, the identification of the vaccine and the amount given. Some vets give a first vaccination at eight weeks, but most dog breeders prefer the course not to commence until about ten weeks because of negating any antibodies passed on by the dam. The vaccination scheduling is usually based on a 15-day cycle. You must take your vet's advice as to when to vaccinate as this may differ according to the vaccine used. Most vaccinations immunize your puppy against viruses.

The usual vaccines contain immunizing doses of several different viruses such as distemper, parvovirus, parainfluenza and hepatitis. There are other vaccines available when the puppy is at risk. You should rely upon professional advice. This is especially true for the booster-shot programme. Most vaccination programmes require a booster when the puppy is a year old and once a year thereafter. In some cases, circumstances may require more frequent immunizations. Kennel cough, more formally known as tracheobronchitis, is treated with a vaccine that is

FEEDING TIPS

Feeding your dog properly is very important. An incorrect diet could affect the dog's health,

behaviour and nervous system, possibly making a normal dog into an aggressive one.

DID YOU KNOW?

Dogs who have been exposed to lawns sprayed with herbicides have double and triple the rate of malignant lymphoma. Town dogs are especially at risk, as they are exposed to tailored lawns and gardens. Dogs perspire and absorb through their footpads. Be careful where your dog walks and always avoid any area that appears yellowed from chemical overspray.

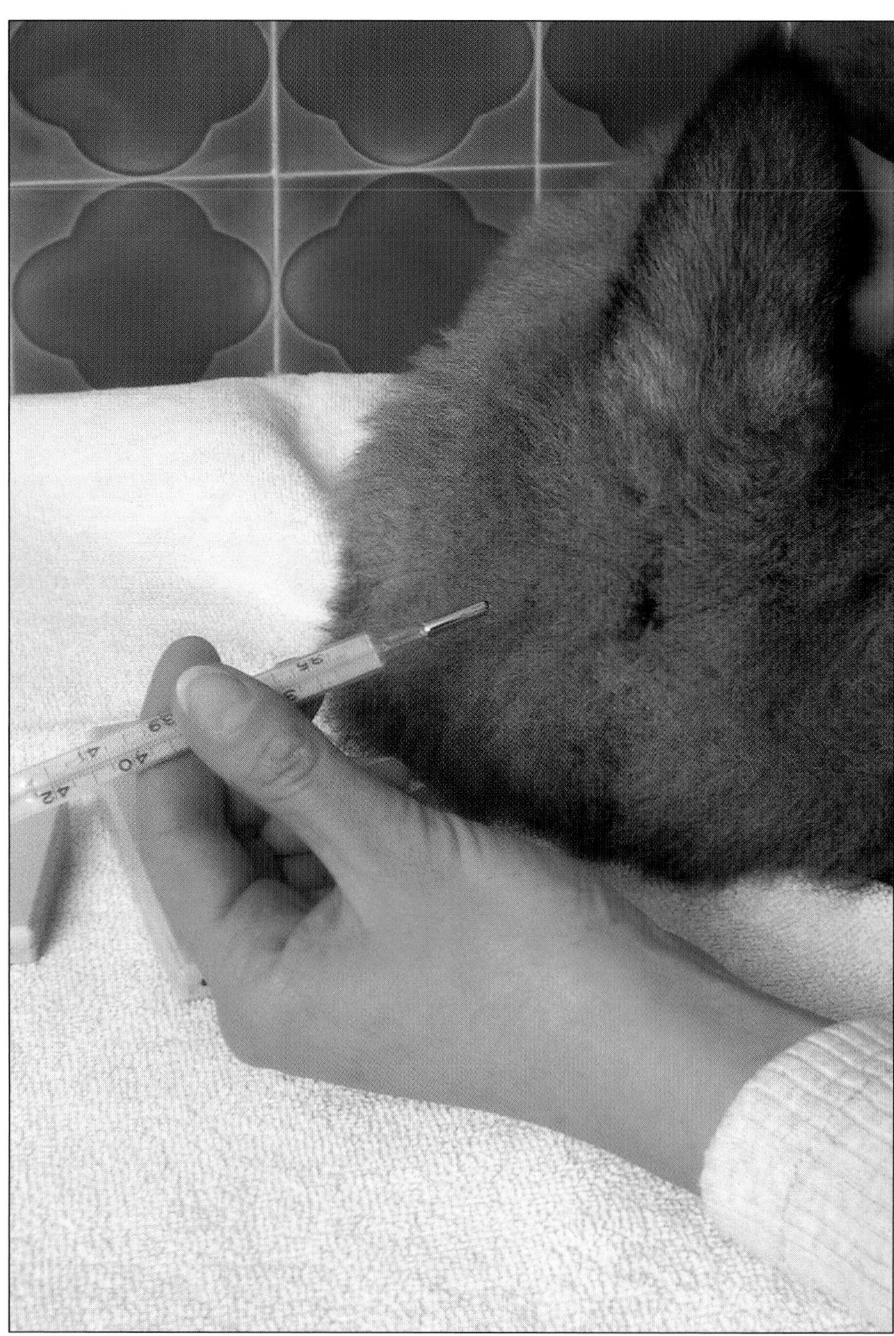

You should learn how to take your Chow's temperature at home.

sprayed into the dog's nostrils. Kennel cough is usually included in routine vaccination, but this is often not so effective as for other major diseases.

Weaning to Five Months Old

Puppies should be weaned by the time they are about two months old. A puppy that remains for at least eight weeks with its mother and litter mates usually adapts better to other dogs and people later in its life.

Some new owners have their puppy examined by a veterinary surgeon immediately, which is a good idea. Vaccination programmes usually begin when the puppy is very young.

The puppy will have its teeth examined and have its skeletal conformation and general health checked prior to certification by the veterinary surgeon. Puppies in certain breeds have problems with their kneecaps, cataracts and other eye problems, heart murmurs and undescended testicles. They may also have personality problems and your veterinary surgeon might have training in temperament evaluation.

KNOW WHEN TO POSTPONE A VACCINATION

Whilst the visit to the vet is costly, it is never advisable to update a vaccination when visiting with a sick or pregnant dog. Vaccinations should be avoided for all elderly dogs. If your dog is showing the signs of any illness or any medical condition, no matter how serious or mild, including skin irritations, do not vaccinate. Likewise, a lame dog should never be vaccinated; and any dog undergoing surgery, or a dog on any immunosuppressant drugs should not be vaccinated until fully recovered.

DID YOU KNOW?

Vaccines do not work all the time. Sometimes dogs are allergic to them and many times the antibodies, which are supposed to be stimulated by the vaccine, just are not produced. You should keep your dog in the veterinary clinic for an hour after it is vaccinated to be sure there are no allergic reactions.

Five Months to One Year of Age

Unless you intend to breed or show your dog, neutering the puppy at six months of age is recommended. Discuss this with your veterinary surgeon; most professionals advise neutering the puppy. Neutering has proven to be extremely beneficial to both male and female puppies. Besides eliminating the possibility of pregnancy, it inhibits (but does not prevent) breast cancer in bitches and prostate cancer in male dogs. Under no circumstances should a bitch be spayed prior to her first season.

HEALTH AND VACCINATION SCHEDULE

AGE IN WEEKS:	6TH	8TH	10TH	12TH	14TH	16TH	20-24TH	1 YR
Worm Control	✔	✔	✔	✔	✔	✔	✔	
Neutering								✔
Heartworm*		✔		✔		✔	✔	
Parvovirus	✔		✔		✔		✔	✔
Distemper		✔		✔		✔		✔
Hepatitis		✔		✔		✔		✔
Leptospirosis								✔
Parainfluenza	✔		✔		✔			✔
Dental Examination		✔					✔	✔
Complete Physical		✔					✔	✔
Coronavirus				✔			✔	✔
Kennel Cough	✔							
Hip Dysplasia								✔
Rabies*							✔	

Vaccinations are not instantly effective. It takes about two weeks for the dog's immunization system to develop antibodies. Most vaccinations require annual booster shots. Your veterinary surgeon should guide you in this regard.

*Not applicable in the United Kingdom

Your veterinary surgeon should provide your puppy with a thorough dental evaluation at six months of age, ascertaining whether all the permanent teeth have erupted properly. A home dental care regimen should be initiated at six months, including brushing weekly and providing good dental devices (such as nylon bones). Regular dental care promotes healthy teeth, fresh breath and a longer life.

ONE TO SEVEN YEARS

Once a year, your grown dog should visit the vet for an examination and vaccination boosters. Some vets recommend blood tests, a thyroid level check and a dental evaluation to accompany these annual visits. A thorough clinical evaluation by the vet can provide critical background information for your dog. Blood tests are often performed at one year of age, and dental examinations around the third or fourth birthday. In the long run, quality preventative care for your pet can save money, teeth and lives.

SKIN PROBLEMS IN CHOW CHOWS

Veterinary surgeons are consulted by dog owners for skin problems more than any other group of diseases or maladies. Dogs' skin is almost as sensitive as human skin and both suffer almost the same ailments (though the occurrence of acne in dogs is rare!). For this reason, veterinary dermatology has developed into a speciality practised by many veterinary surgeons.

Since many skin problems have visual symptoms that are almost identical, it requires the skill of an experienced veterinary dermatologist to identify and cure many of the more severe skin disorders. Pet shops sell many treatments for skin problems but most of the treatments are directed at symptoms and not the underlying problem(s). If your dog is suffering from a skin disorder, you should seek professional assistance as quickly as possible. As with all diseases, the earlier a problem is identified and treated, the more successful is the cure.

Hereditary Skin Disorders

Veterinary dermatologists are currently researching a number of

DISEASE REFERENCE CHART

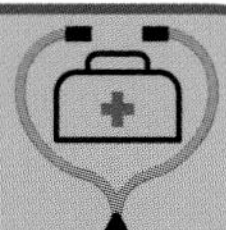

	What is it?	What causes it?	Symptoms
Leptospirosis	Severe disease that affects the internal organs; can be spread to people.	A bacterium, which is often carried by rodents, that enters through mucous membranes and spreads quickly throughout the body.	Range from fever, vomiting and loss of appetite in less severe cases to shock, irreversible kidney damage and possibly death in most severe cases.
Rabies	Potentially deadly virus that infects warm-blooded mammals. Not seen in United Kingdom.	Bite from a carrier of the virus, mainly wild animals.	1st stage: dog exhibits change in behaviour, fear. 2nd stage: dog's behaviour becomes more aggressive. 3rd stage: loss of coordination, trouble with bodily functions.
Parvovirus	Highly contagious virus, potentially deadly.	Ingestion of the virus, which is usually spread through the faeces of infected dogs.	Most common: severe diarrhoea. Also vomiting, fatigue, lack of appetite.
Kennel cough	Contagious respiratory infection.	Combination of types of bacteria and virus. Most common: *Bordetella bronchiseptica* bacteria and parainfluenza virus.	Chronic cough.
Distemper	Disease primarily affecting respiratory and nervous system.	Virus that is related to the human measles virus.	Mild symptoms such as fever, lack of appetite and mucous secretion progress to evidence of brain damage, 'hard pad.'
Hepatitis	Virus primarily affecting the liver.	Canine adenovirus type I (CAV-1). Enters system when dog breathes in particles.	Lesser symptoms include listlessness, diarrhoea, vomiting. More severe symptoms include 'blue-eye' (clumps of virus in eye).
Coronavirus	Virus resulting in digestive problems.	Virus is spread through infected dog's faeces.	Stomach upset evidenced by lack of appetite, vomiting, diarrhoea.

Normal hairs of a dog enlarged 200 times original size. The cuticle (outer covering) is clean and healthy. Unlike human hair that grows from the base, dog's hair also grows from the end, as shown in the inset. Scanning electron micrographs by Dr Dennis Kunkel, University of Hawaii.

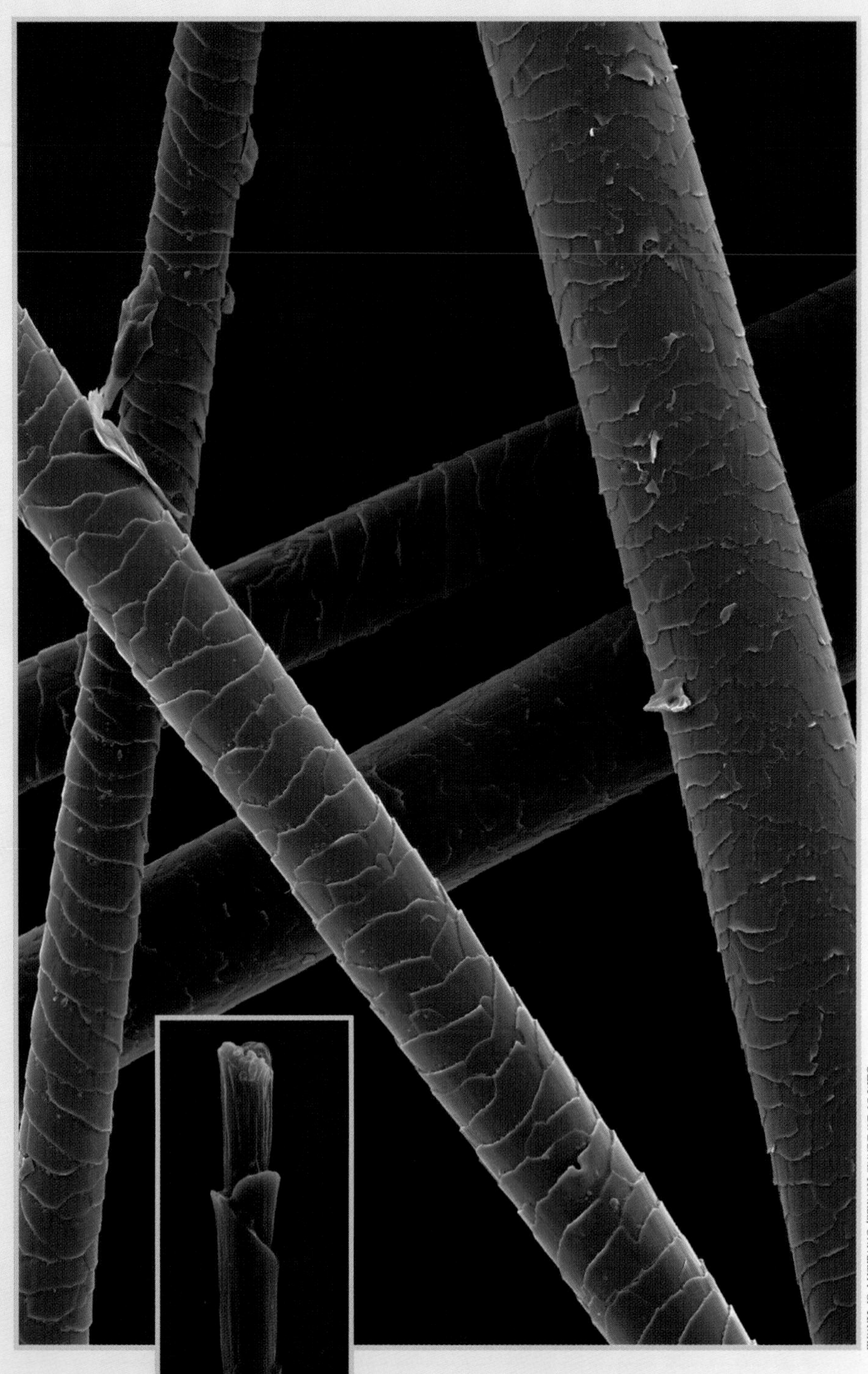

SEM BY DR DENNIS KUNKEL, UNIVERSITY OF HAWAII

A SKUNKY PROBLEM

Have you noticed your dog dragging his rump along the floor? If so, it is likely that his anal sacs are impacted or possibly infected. The anal sacs are small pouches located on both sides of the anus under the skin and muscles. They are about the size and shape of a grape and contain a foul-smelling liquid. Their contents are usually emptied when the dog has a bowel movement, but if they are not emptied completely, they will impact, which will cause your dog a lot of pain. Fortunately, your veterinary surgeon can tend to this problem easily by draining the sacs for the dog. Be aware that your dog might also empty his anal sacs in cases of extreme fright.

skin disorders that are believed to have a hereditary basis. These inherited diseases are transmitted by both parents, who appear (phenotypically) normal but have a recessive gene for the disease, meaning that they carry, but are not affected by, the disease. These diseases pose serious problems to breeders because in some instances there is no method of identifying carriers. Often the secondary diseases associated with these skin conditions are even more debilitating than the skin disorder, including cancers and respiratory problems; others can be lethal.

Amongst the known hereditary skin disorders, for which the mode of inheritance is known, are acrodermatitis, cutaneous asthenia (Ehlers-Danlos syndrome), sebaceous adenitis, cyclic hematopoiesis, dermatomyositis, IgA deficiency, colour dilution alopecia and nodular dermatofibrosis. Some of these disorders are limited to one or two breeds and others affect a large number of breeds. Reports of both sebaceous adenitis and colour dilution alopecia are known for the Chow Chow. All inherited diseases must be diagnosed and treated by a veterinary specialist.

Parasite Bites

Many of us are allergic to insect bites. The bites itch, erupt and may even become infected. Dogs have the same reaction to fleas, ticks and/or mites. When an insect lands on you, you have the chance to whisk it away with your hand. Unfortunately, when our dog is bitten by a flea, tick or mite, it can only scratch it away

DID YOU KNOW?

Your veterinary surgeon will probably recommend that your puppy be vaccinated before you take him outside. There are airborne diseases, parasite eggs in the grass and unexpected visits from other dogs that might be dangerous to your puppy's health.

PARVO FOR THE COURSE

Canine parvovirus is a highly contagious disease that attacks puppies and older dogs. Spread through contact with infected faeces, parvovirus causes bloody diarrhoea, vomiting, heart damage, dehydration, shock and death. To prevent this tragedy, have your puppy begin his series of vaccinations at six to eight weeks. Be aware that the virus is easily spread and is carried on a dog's hair and feet, water bowls and other objects, as well as people's shoes and clothing.

or bite it. By the time the dog has been bitten, the parasite has done some of its damage. It may also have laid eggs to cause further problems in the near future. The itching from parasite bites is probably due to the saliva injected into the site when the parasite sucks the dog's blood.

AUTO-IMMUNE SKIN CONDITIONS

Auto-immune skin conditions are commonly referred to as being allergic to yourself, while allergies are usually inflammatory reactions to an outside stimulus. Auto-immune diseases cause serious damage to the tissues that are involved.

The best known auto-immune disease is lupus, which affects people as well as dogs. The symptoms are variable and may affect the kidneys, bones, blood chemistry and skin. It can be fatal to both dogs and humans, though it is not thought to be transmissible. It is usually successfully treated with cortisone, prednisone or a similar corticosteroid, but extensive use of these drugs can have harmful side effects.

HOT SPOTS

Hot spots are localized patches of inflamed skin that are related to 'Staph' infections. The bacterium that causes these infections, *Staphylococcus*, is normally present on dogs, and other animals, and is not contagious. When the dog's immune system is compromised, usually by stress caused by change in environment, weather or emotion, the Staph infection develops. The dog will lick and bite at an area to the point that it becomes infected and pus-covered. Vets treat these hot spots but are usually concerned

'P' STANDS FOR PROBLEM

Urinary tract disease is a serious condition that requires immediate medical attention. Symptoms include urinating in inappropriate places or the need to urinate frequently in small amounts. Urinary tract disease is most effectively treated with antibiotics. To help promote good urinary tract health, owners must always be sure that a constant supply of fresh water is available to their pets.

First Aid at a Glance

Burns
Place the affected area under cool water; use ice if only a small area is burnt.

Bee/Insect bites
Apply ice to relieve swelling; antihistamine dosed properly.

Animal bites
Clean any bleeding area; apply pressure until bleeding subsides; go to the vet.

Spider bites
Use cold compress and a pressurised pack to inhibit venom's spreading.

Antifreeze poisoning
Induce vomiting with hydrogen peroxide. Seek *immediate* veterinary help!

Fish hooks
Removal best handled by vet; hook must be cut in order to remove.

Snake bites
Pack ice around bite; contact vet quickly; identify snake for proper antivenin.

Car accident
Move dog from roadway with blanket; seek veterinary aid.

Shock
Calm the dog, keep him warm; seek immediate veterinary help.

Nosebleed
Apply cold compress to the nose; apply pressure to any visible abrasion.

Bleeding
Apply pressure above the area; treat wound by applying a cotton pack.

Heat stroke
Submerge dog in cold bath; cool down with fresh air and water; go to the vet.

Frostbite/Hypothermia
Warm the dog with a warm bath, electric blankets or hot water bottles.

Abrasions
Clean the wound and wash out thoroughly with fresh water; apply antiseptic.

Remember: an injured dog may attempt to bite a helping hand from fear and confusion. Always muzzle the dog before trying to offer assistance.

CANINE DENTAL CARE

A dental examination is in order when the dog is between six months and one year of age so any permanent teeth that have erupted incorrectly can be corrected. It is important to begin a brushing routine, preferably using a two-sided brushing technique, whereby both sides of the tooth are

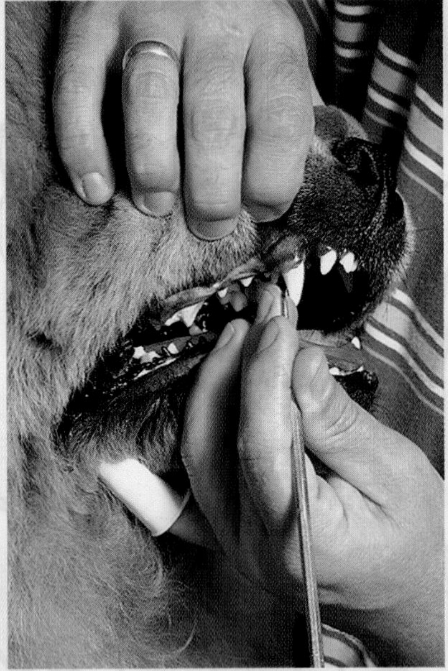

brushed at the same time. Durable nylon and safe edible chews should be a part of your puppy's arsenal for good health, good teeth and pleasant breath. The vast majority of dogs three to four years old and older has diseases of the gums from lack of dental attention. Using the various types of dental chews can be very effective in controlling dental plaque.

about the underlying cause. With recurrent infections, possible causes are hypothyroidism, seborrheic skin conditions, hereditary immune disorders, as well as inhalant or food allergies. Antibiotics are a common therapy, which prove effective in clearing up the hot spot. Boosting the dog's immune system should be discussed with the vet as a possible way of rectifying the recurrent problem.

With coated breeds such as the Chow Chow, hot spots often occur in the summer months. Dogs tend to bite their tails and/or rear quarters. Some hot spots may be 'coat related', and proper grooming and bathing/drying techniques are important to avoid summer skin problems.

Airborne Allergies

Another interesting allergy is pollen allergy. Humans have hay fever, rose fever and other fevers with which they suffer during the pollinating season. Many dogs suffer the same allergies. When the pollen count is high, your dog might suffer but don't expect them to sneeze and have runny noses like humans. Dogs react to pollen allergies the same way they react to fleas—they scratch and bite themselves.

Dogs, like humans, can be tested for allergens. Discuss the testing with your veterinary dermatologist.

FOOD PROBLEMS

Food Allergies

Dogs are allergic to many foods that are best-sellers and highly recommended by breeders and veterinary surgeons. Changing the brand of food that you buy may not eliminate the problem if the element to which the dog is allergic is contained in the new brand.

Recognising a food allergy is difficult. Humans vomit or have rashes when they eat a food to which they are allergic. Dogs neither vomit nor (usually) develop a rash. They react in the same manner as they do to an airborne or flea allergy; they itch, scratch and bite. This makes the diagnosis extremely difficult. While pollen allergies and parasite bites are usually seasonal, food allergies are year-round problems.

Food Intolerance

Food intolerance is the inability of the dog to completely digest certain foods. Puppies that may have done very well on their mother's milk may not do well on cow's milk. The result of this food intolerance may be loose bowels, passing gas and stomach pains. These are the only obvious symptoms of food intolerance, which makes diagnosis difficult.

Treating Food Problems

It is possible to handle food allergies and food intolerance yourself. Put your dog on a diet that it has never had. Obviously if it has never eaten this new food it can't have been allergic or intolerant of it. Start with a single ingredient that is not in the dog's diet at the present time. Ingredients like chopped beef or fish are common in dogs' diets, so try something more exotic like rabbit, pheasant or even just vegetables. Keep the dog on this diet (with no additives) for a month. If the symptoms of food allergy or intolerance disappear, chances are your dog has a food allergy.

Don't think that the single ingredient cured the problem. You still must find a suitable diet and ascertain which ingredient in the old diet was objectionable. This is most easily done by adding ingredients to the new diet one at a time. Let the dog stay on the modified diet for a month before you add another ingredient. Eventually, you will determine the ingredient that caused the adverse reaction.

An alternative method is to study the ingredients in the diet to which your dog is allergic or intolerant. Identify the main ingredient in this diet and eliminate the main ingredient by buying a different food that does not have that ingredient. Keep experimenting until the symptoms disappear.

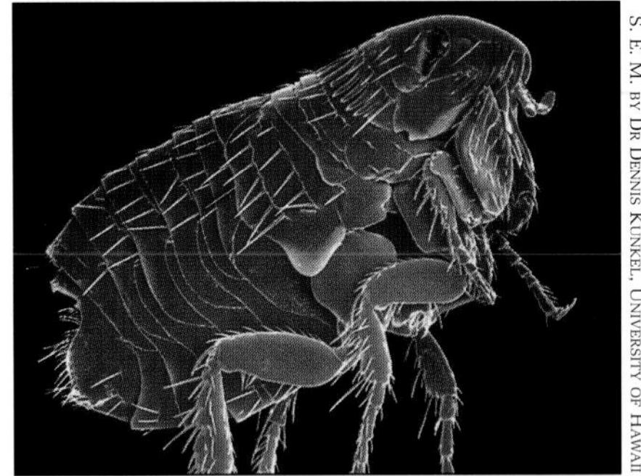

A scanning electron micrograph (S. E. M.) of a dog flea, *Ctenocephalides canis.*

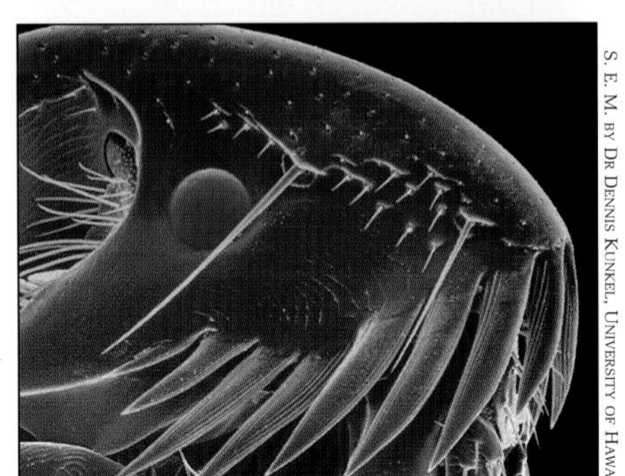

Magnified head of a dog flea, *Ctenocephalides canis.*

EXTERNAL PARASITES

Of all the problems to which dogs are prone, none is more well known and frustrating than fleas. Flea infestation is relatively simple to cure but difficult to prevent. Parasites that are harboured inside the body are a bit more difficult to eradicate but they are easier to control.

FLEAS

To control a flea infestation you have to understand the flea's life cycle. Fleas are often thought of as a summertime problem but centrally heated homes have changed the patterns and fleas can be found at any time of the year. The most effective method of flea control is a two-stage approach:

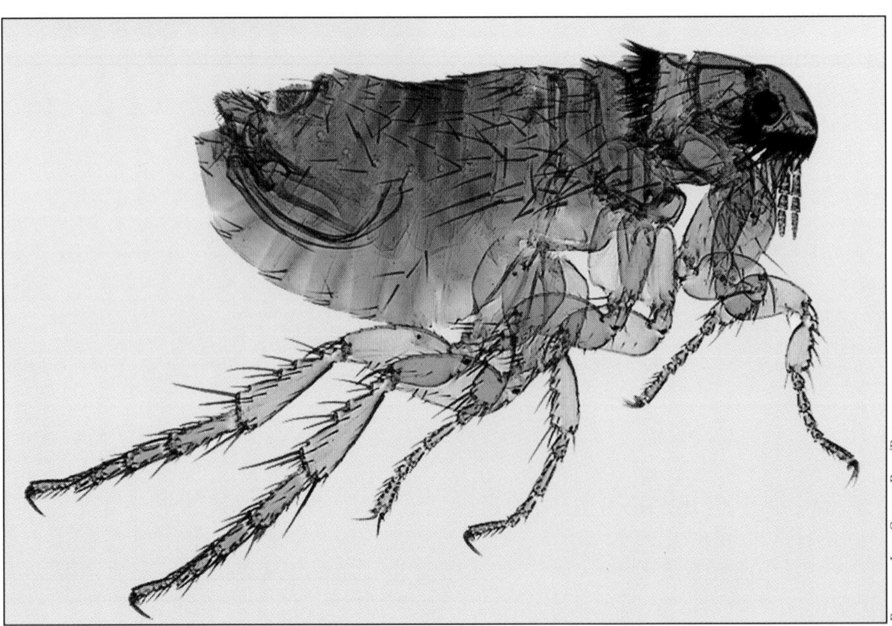

A male dog flea, *Ctenocephalides canis.*

DID YOU KNOW?

Flea-killers are poisonous. You should not spray these toxic chemicals on areas of a dog's body that he licks, on his genitals or on his face. Flea killers taken internally are a better answer, but check with your vet in case internal therapy is not advised for your dog.

one stage to kill the adult fleas, and the other to control the development of pre-adult fleas. Unfortunately, no single active ingredient is effective against all stages of the life cycle.

Life Cycle Stages

During its life, a flea will pass through four life stages: egg, larva, pupa and adult. The adult stage is the most visible and irritating stage of the flea life cycle and this is why the majority of flea-control products concentrate on this stage. The fact is that adult fleas account for only 1% of the total flea population, and the other 99% exist in pre-adult stages, i.e. eggs, larvae and pupae. The pre-adult stages are barely visible to the naked eye.

The Life Cycle of the Flea

Eggs are laid on the dog, usually in quantities of about 20 or 30, several times a day. The female adult flea must have a blood meal before each egg-laying session. When first laid, the eggs will cling to the dog's fur, as the eggs are still moist. However, they will quickly dry out and fall from the dog, especially if the dog moves around or scratches. Many eggs will fall off in the dog's favourite area or an area in which he spends a lot of time, such as his bed.

Once the eggs fall from the dog onto the carpet or furniture, they will hatch into larvae. This takes from one to ten days. Larvae are not particularly mobile, and will usually travel only a few inches from where they hatch. However, they do have a tendency to move

A Look at Fleas

Fleas have been around for millions of years and have adapted to changing host animals. They are able to go through a complete life cycle in less than one month or they can extend their lives to almost two years by remaining as pupae or cocoons. They do not need blood or any other food for up to 20 months.

They have been measured as being able to jump 300,000 times and can jump 150 times their length in any direction including straight up. Those are just a few of the reasons why they are so successful in infesting a dog!

Illustration Courtesy of Bayer Vital GmbH & Co. KG

away from light and heavy traffic—under furniture and behind doors are common places to find high quantities of flea larvae.

The flea larvae feed on dead organic matter, including adult flea faeces, until they are ready to change into adult fleas. Fleas will usually remain as larvae for around seven days. After this period, the larvae will pupate into protective pupae. While inside the pupae, the larvae will undergo metamorphosis and change into adult fleas. This can take as little time as a few days, but the adult fleas can remain inside the pupae waiting to hatch for up to two years. The pupae are signalled to hatch by certain stimuli, such as physical pressure—the pupae's being stepped on, heat from an animal lying on the pupae or increased carbon dioxide levels and vibrations—indicating that a suitable host is available.

Once hatched, the adult flea must feed within a few days. Once the adult flea finds a host, it will not leave voluntarily. It only becomes dislodged by grooming or the host animal's scratching. The adult flea will remain on the host for the duration of its life unless forcibly removed.

EN GARDE: CATCHING FLEAS OFF GUARD

Consider the following ways to arm yourself against fleas:

- Add a small amount of pennyroyal or eucalyptus oil to your dog's bath. These natural remedies repel fleas.
- Supplement your dog's food with fresh garlic (minced or grated) and a hearty amount of brewer's yeast, both of which ward off fleas.
- Use a flea comb on your dog daily. Submerge fleas in a cup of bleach to kill them quickly.
- Confine the dog to only a few rooms to limit the spread of fleas in the home.
- Vacuum daily...and get all of the crevices! Dispose of the bag every few days until the problem is under control.
- Wash your dog's bedding daily. Cover cushions where your dog sleeps with towels, and wash the towels often.

DID YOU KNOW?

Never mix flea control products without first consulting your veterinary surgeon. Some products can become toxic when combined with others and can cause serious or fatal consequences.

TREATING THE ENVIRONMENT AND THE DOG

Treating fleas should be a two-pronged attack. First, the environment needs to be treated; this includes carpets and furniture, especially the dog's bedding and

Opposite page: A scanning electron micrograph of a dog or cat flea, *Ctenocephalides*, magnified more than 100x. This image has been colourized for effect.

The Life Cycle of the Flea

Adult

Egg

Larva

Pupa

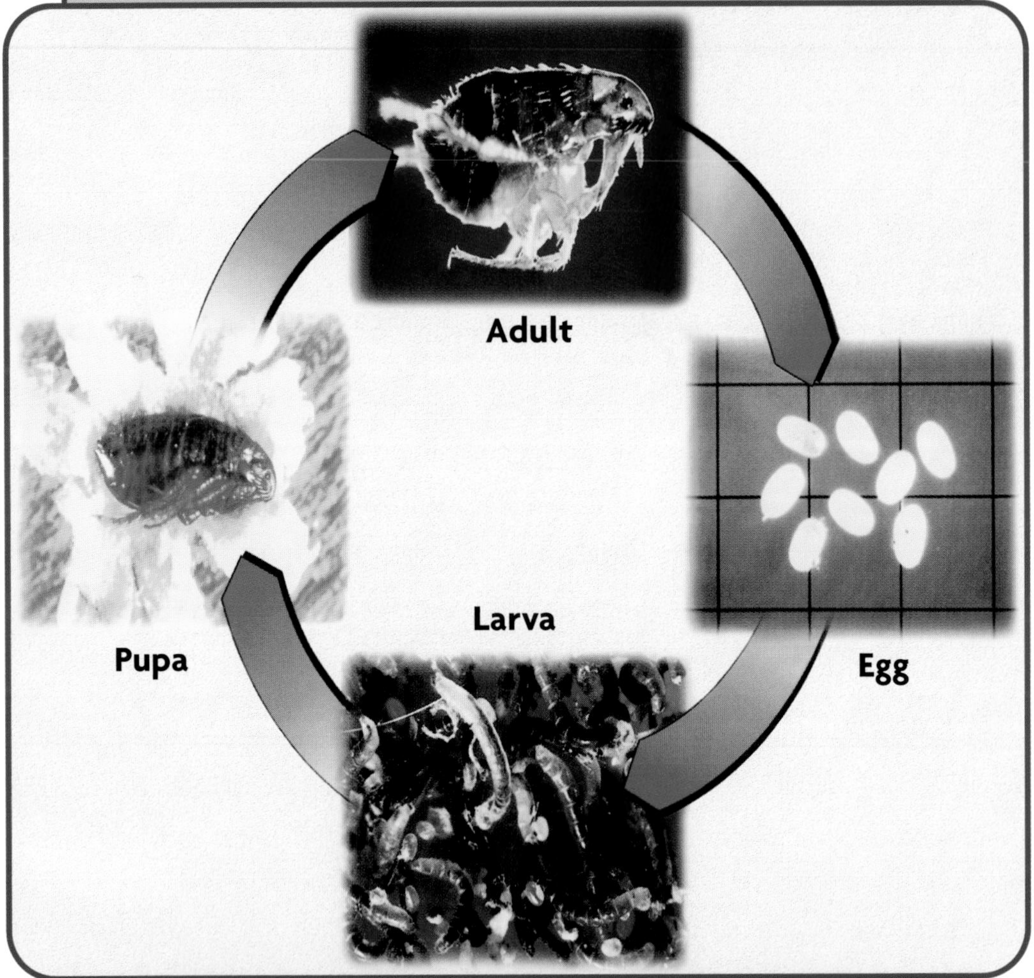

This graphic depiction of the life cycle of the flea appears courtesy of Fleabusters®, R_x for fleas.

areas underneath furniture. The environment should be treated with a household spray containing an Insect Growth Regulator (IGR) and an insecticide to kill the adult fleas. Most IGRs are effective against eggs and larvae; they actually mimic the fleas' own hormones and stop the eggs and larvae from developing into adult fleas. There are currently no treatments available to attack the pupa stage of the life cycle, so the adult insecticide is used to kill the newly hatched adult fleas before

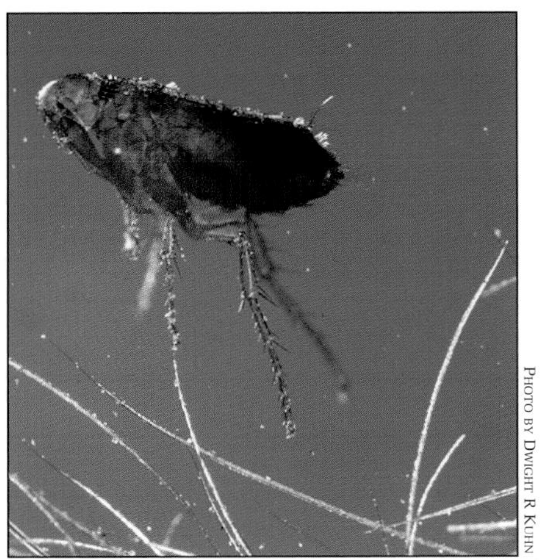
PHOTO BY DWIGHT R KUHN

Dwight R Kuhn's magnificent action photo showing a flea jumping from a dog's back.

they find a host. Most IGRs are active for many months, whilst adult insecticides are only active for a few days.

When treating with a household spray, it is a good idea to vacuum before applying the product. This stimulates as many pupae as possible to hatch into adult fleas. The vacuum cleaner should also be treated with a flea treatment to prevent the eggs and larvae that have been hoovered into the vacuum bag from hatching.

The second stage of treatment is to apply an adult insecticide to the dog. Traditionally, this would be in the form of a collar or a spray, but more recent innovations include digestible insecticides that poison the fleas when they ingest the dog's blood. Alternatively, there are drops that, when placed on the back of the animal's neck, spread throughout the fur and skin to kill adult fleas.

TICKS AND MITES

Though not as common as fleas, ticks and mites are found all over the tropical and temperate world. They don't bite, like fleas; they harpoon. They dig their sharp proboscis (nose) into the dog's skin and drink the blood. Their only food and drink is dog's blood. Dogs can get Lyme disease, Rocky Mountain spotted fever (normally

FLEA CONTROL

Two types of products should be used when treating fleas—a product to treat the pet and a product to treat the home. Adult fleas represent less than 1% of the flea population. The pre-adult fleas (eggs, larvae and pupae) represent more than 99% of the flea population and are found in the environment; it is in the case of pre-adult fleas that products containing an Insect Growth Regulator (IGR) should be used in the home.

IGRs are a new class of compounds used to prevent the development of insects. They do not kill the insect outright, but instead use the insect's biology against it to stop it from completing its growth. Products that contain methoprene are the world's first and leading IGRs. Used to control fleas and other insects, this type of IGR will stop flea larvae from developing and protect the house for up to seven months.

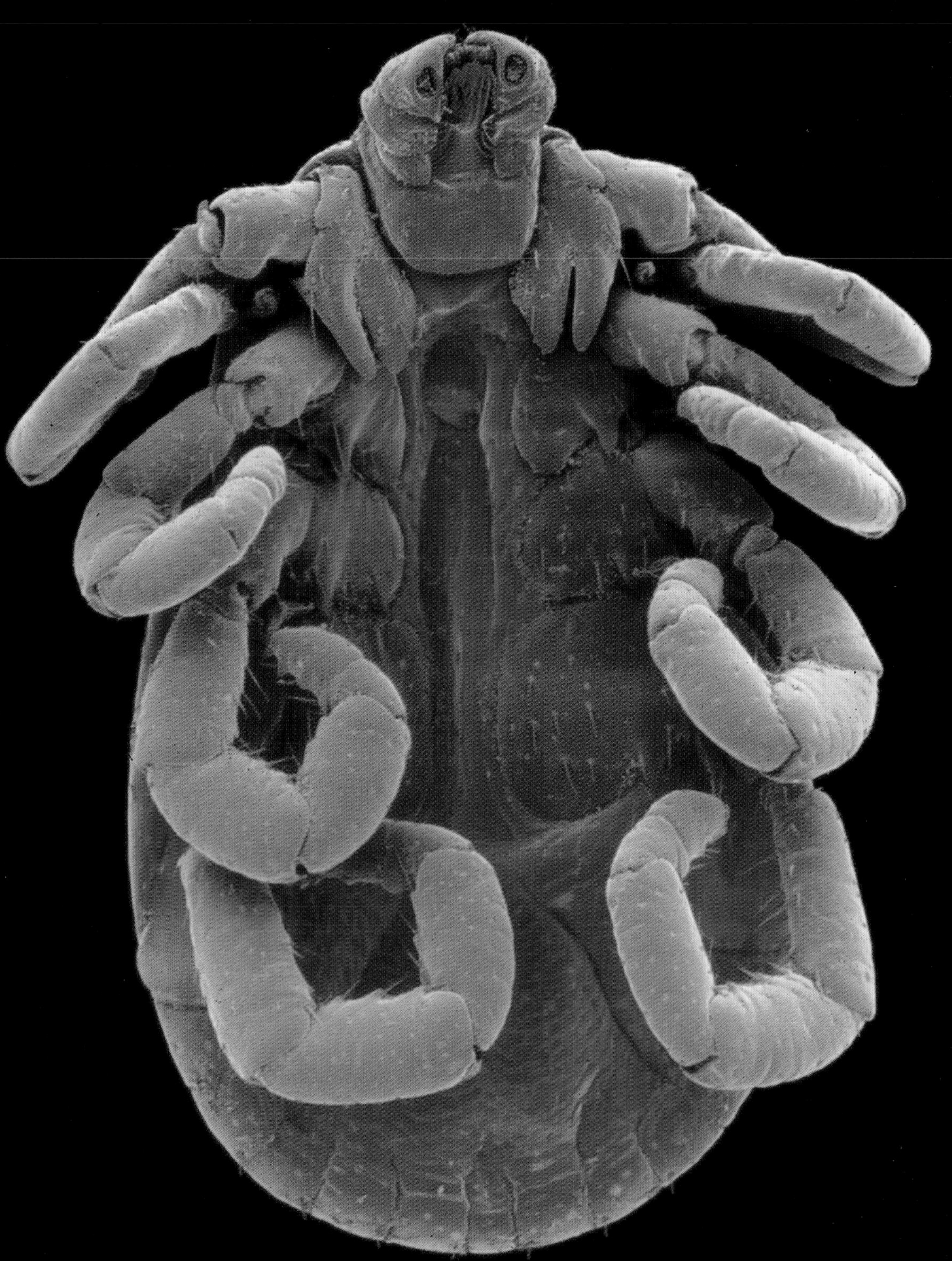

found in the US only), paralysis and many other diseases from ticks and mites. They may live where fleas are found and they like to hide in cracks or seams in walls wherever dogs live. They are controlled the same way fleas are controlled.

The dog tick, *Dermacentor variabilis*, may well be the most common dog tick in many geographical areas, especially those areas where the climate is hot and humid.

Most dog ticks have life expectancies of a week to six

S. E. M. by Dr Dennis Kunkel University of Hawaii

Beware the Deer Tick

The great outdoors may be fun for your dog, but it also is a home to dangerous ticks. Deer ticks carry a bacterium known as *Borrelia burgdorferi* and are most active in the autumn and spring. When infections are caught early, penicillin and tetracycline are effective antibiotics, but if left untreated the bacteria may cause neurological, kidney and cardiac problems as well as long-term trouble with walking and painful joints.

Illustration Courtesy of Bayer Vital GmbH & Co. KG

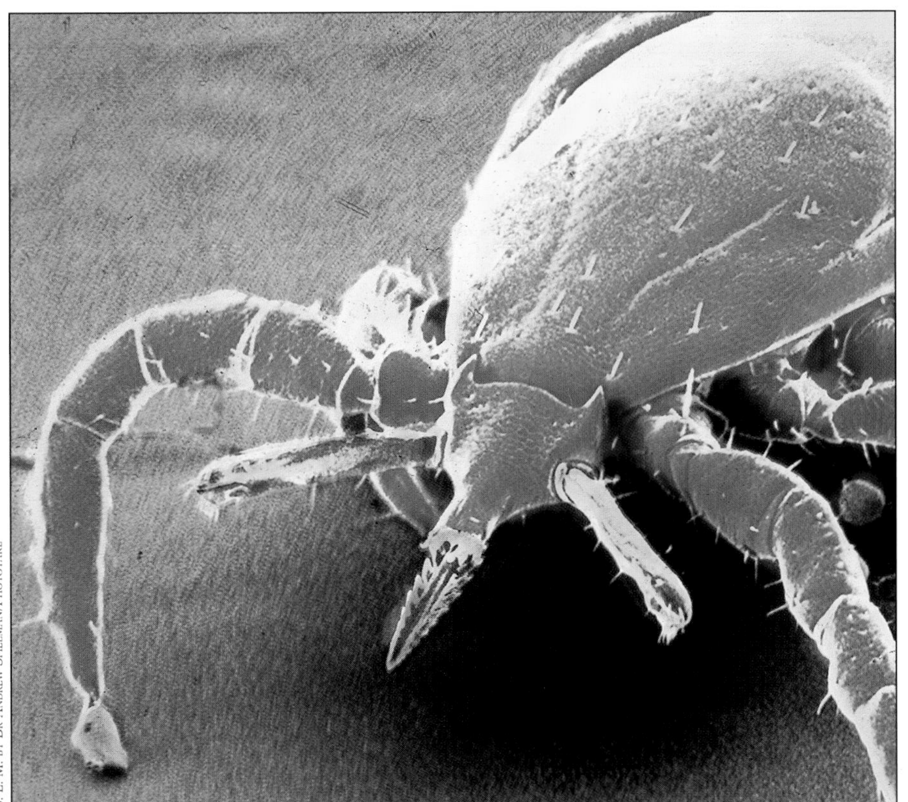

S. E. M. by Dr Andrew Spielman/Phototake

A deer tick, the carrier of Lyme disease. This magnified micrograph has been colourized for effect.

Opposite page: The dog tick, *Dermacentor variabilis*, is probably the most common tick found on dogs. Look at the strength in its eight legs! No wonder it's hard to detach them.

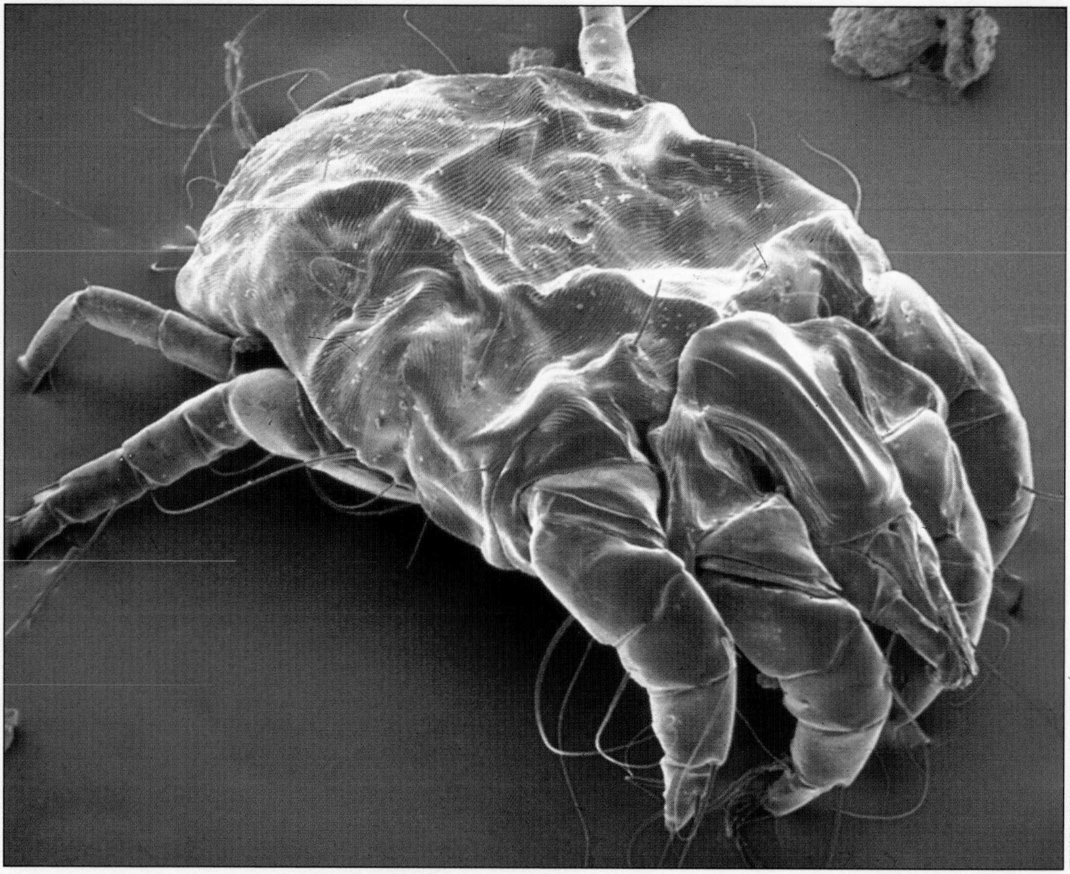

PHOTO BY JAMES HAYDEN-YOAV/PHOTOTAKE.

Above:
The mange mite,
Psoroptes bovis.

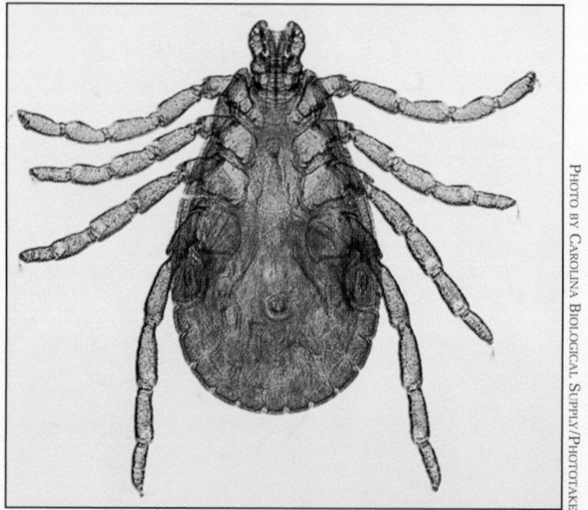

PHOTO BY CAROLINA BIOLOGICAL SUPPLY/PHOTOTAKE

A brown dog tick, *Rhipicephalus sanguineus*, is an uncommon but annoying tick found on dogs.

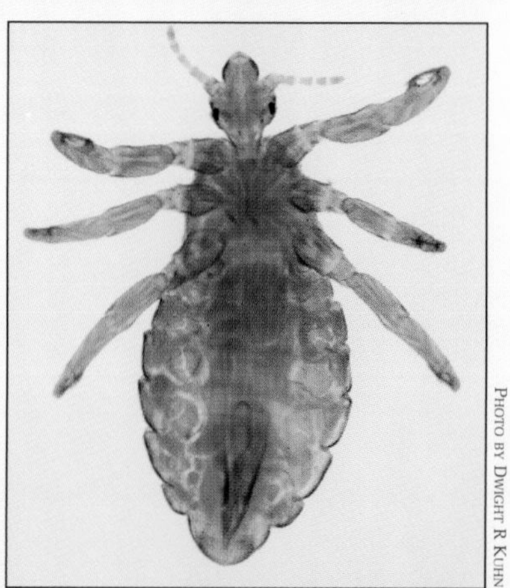

PHOTO BY DWIGHT R KUHN

Human lice look like dog lice; the two are closely related

months, depending upon climatic conditions. They can neither jump nor fly, but they can crawl slowly and can range up to 5 metres (16 feet) to reach a sleeping or unsuspecting dog.

MANGE

Mites cause a skin irritation called mange. Some are contagious, like *Cheyletiella*, ear mites, scabies and chiggers. Mites that cause ear-mite infestations are usually controlled with Lindane, which can only be administered by a vet, followed by Tresaderm at home.

It is essential that your dog be treated for mange as quickly as possible because some forms of mange are transmissible to people.

INTERNAL PARASITES

Most animals—fishes, birds and mammals, including dogs and humans—have worms and other parasites that live inside their bodies. According to Dr Herbert R Axelrod, the fish pathologist, there are two kinds of parasites: dumb and smart. The smart parasites live in peaceful cooperation with their hosts (symbiosis), while the dumb parasites kill their host. Most of the worm infections are relatively easy to control. If they are not controlled they weaken the host dog to the point that other medical problems occur, but they are not dumb parasites.

ROUNDWORMS

The roundworms that infect dogs are scientifically known as *Toxocara canis*. They live in the dog's intestine. The worms shed eggs continually. It has been estimated that a dog produces about 150 grammes of faeces every day. Each gramme of faeces averages 10,000–12,000 eggs of roundworms. There are no known areas in which dogs roam that do not contain roundworm eggs. The greatest danger of roundworms is that they infect people too! It is

DEWORMING

Ridding your puppy of worms is VERY IMPORTANT because certain worms that puppies carry, such as tapeworms and roundworms, can infect humans.

Breeders initiate a deworming programme at or about four weeks of age. The routine is repeated every two or three weeks until the puppy is three months old. The breeder from whom you obtained your puppy should provide you with the complete details of the deworming programme.

Your veterinary surgeon can prescribe and monitor the programme of deworming for you. The usual programme is treating the puppy every 15–20 days until the puppy is positively worm free.

It is not advised that you treat your puppy with drugs that are not recommended professionally.

wise to have your dog tested regularly for roundworms.

Pigs also have roundworm infections that can be passed to humans and dogs. The typical roundworm parasite is called *Ascaris lumbricoides*.

Hookworms

The worm *Ancylostoma caninum* is commonly called the dog hookworm. It is dangerous to humans and cats. It also has teeth by which it attaches itself to the intestines of the dog. It changes the site of its attachment about six times a day and the dog loses blood from each detachment, possibly causing iron-deficiency anaemia. Hookworms are easily purged from the dog with many medications. Milbemycin oxime,

ROUNDWORMS

Average size dogs can pass 1,360,000 roundworm eggs every day.

For example, if there were only 1 million dogs in the world, the world would be saturated with 1,300 metric tonnes of dog faeces.

These faeces would contain 15,000,000,000 roundworm eggs.

It's known that 7–31% of home gardens and children's play boxes in the US contain roundworm eggs.

Flushing dog's faeces down the toilet is not a safe practice because the usual sewage treatments do not destroy roundworm eggs.

Infected puppies start shedding roundworm eggs at 3 weeks of age. They can be infected by their mother's milk.

The roundworm, *Rhabditis*. The roundworm can infect both dogs and humans.

Photo by Carolina Biological Supply/Phototake

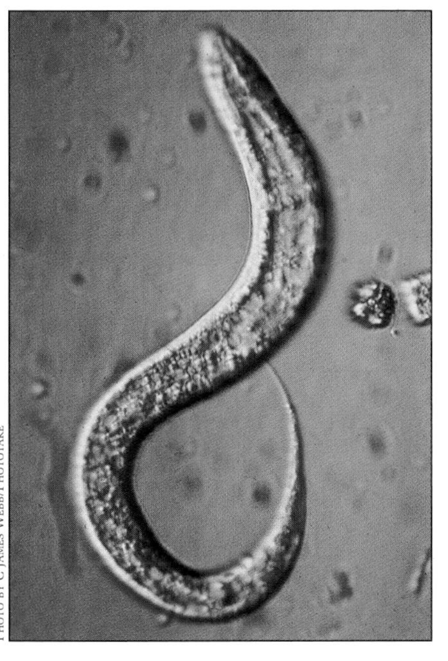

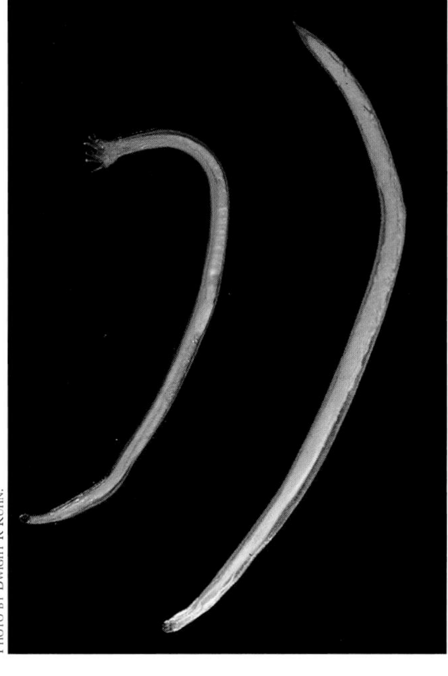

Left:
The infective stage of the hookworm larva.

Right:
Male and female hookworms, *Ancylostoma caninum*, are uncommonly found in pet or show dogs in Britain. Hookworms may infect other dogs that have exposure to grasslands.

which also serves as a heartworm preventative in Collies, can be used for this purpose.

In Britain the 'temperate climate' hookworm (*Uncinaria stenocephala*) is rarely found in pet or show dogs, but can occur in hunting packs, racing Greyhounds and sheepdogs because the worms can be prevalent wherever dogs are exercised regularly on grassland.

DID YOU KNOW?

Never allow your dog to swim in polluted water or public areas where water quality can be suspect. Even perfectly clear water can harbour parasites, many of which can cause serious to fatal illnesses in canines. Areas inhabited by waterfowl and other wildlife are especially dangerous.

TAPEWORMS

There are many species of tapeworms. They are carried by fleas! The dog eats the flea and starts the tapeworm cycle. Humans can also be infected with tapeworms, so don't eat fleas! Fleas are so small that your dog could pass them onto your hands, your plate or your food and thus make it possible for you to ingest a flea which is carrying tapeworm eggs.

While tapeworm infection is not life threatening in dogs (smart parasite!), it can be the cause of a

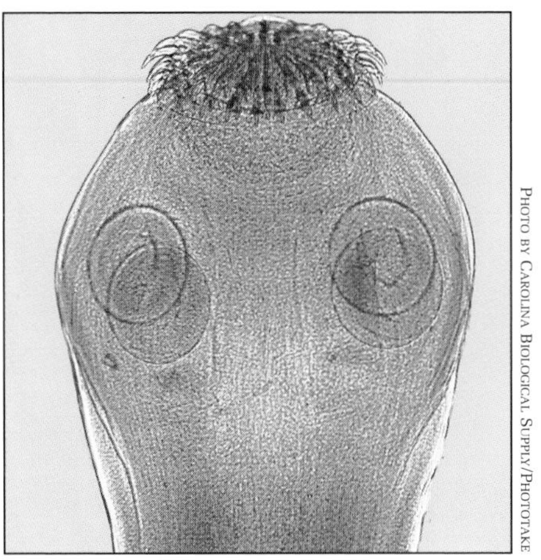

The head and rostellum (the round prominence on the scolex) of a tapeworm, which infects dogs and humans.

PHOTO BY CAROLINA BIOLOGICAL SUPPLY/PHOTOTAKE

very serious liver disease for humans. About 50 percent of the humans infected with *Echinococcus multilocularis*, a type of tapeworm that causes alveolar hydatis, perish.

HEARTWORMS

Heartworms are thin, extended worms up to 30 cms (12 ins) long which live in a dog's heart and the major blood vessels surrounding it. Dogs may have up to 200 worms. Symptoms may be loss of energy, loss of appetite, coughing, the development of a pot belly and anaemia.

Heartworms are transmitted by mosquitoes. The mosquito drinks the blood of an infected dog and takes in larvae with the blood. The larvae, called microfilaria, develop within the body of the mosquito and are passed on to the next dog bitten after the larvae mature. It takes two to three weeks for the larvae to develop to the infective stage within the body of the mosquito. Dogs should be treated at about six weeks of age, and maintained on a prophylactic dose given monthly.

Blood testing for heartworms is not necessarily indicative of how seriously your dog is infected. This is a dangerous disease. Although heartworm is a problem for dogs in America, Australia, Asia and Central Europe, dogs in the United Kingdom are not currently affected by heartworm.

TAPEWORMS

Humans, rats, squirrels, foxes, coyotes, wolves, mixed breeds of dogs and purebred dogs are all susceptible to tapeworm infection. Except in humans, tapeworms are usually not a fatal infection.

Infected individuals can harbour a thousand parasitic worms.

Tapeworms have two sexes—male and female (many other worms have only one sex—male and female in the same worm).

If dogs eat infected rats or mice, they get the tapeworm disease.

One month after attaching to a dog's intestine, the worm starts shedding eggs. These eggs are infective immediately.

Infective eggs can live for a few months without a host animal.

Roundworms, whipworms and hookworms are just a few of the other commonly known worms that infect dogs.

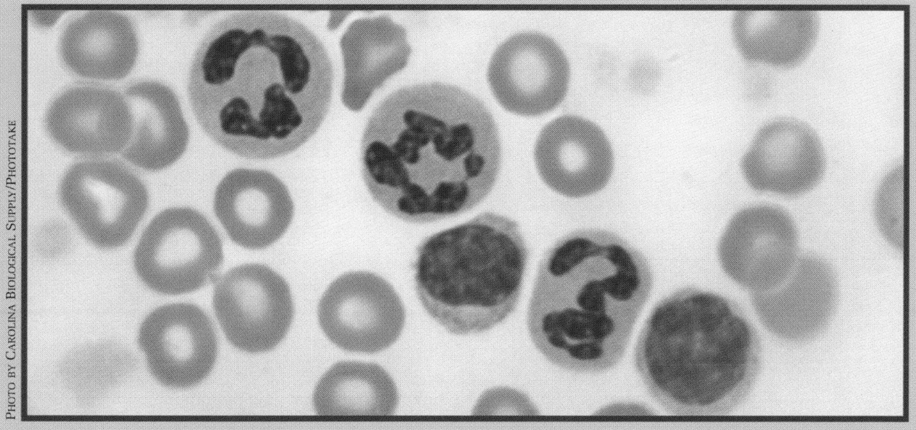
PHOTO BY CAROLINA BIOLOGICAL SUPPLY/PHOTOTAKE

Magnified heartworm larvae, *Dirofilaria immitis.*

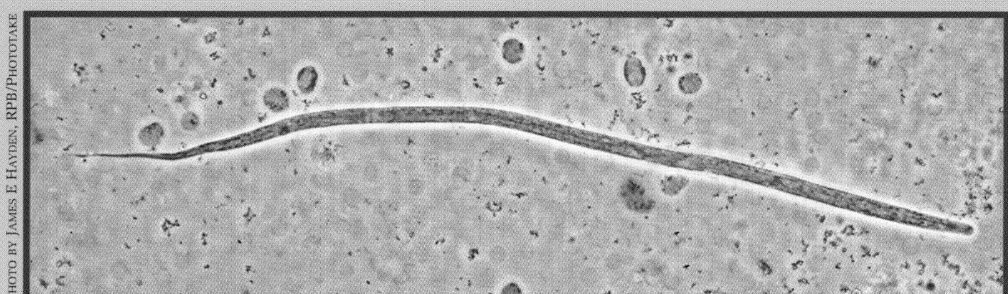
PHOTO BY JAMES E HAYDEN, RPB/PHOTOTAKE

The heartworm, *Dirofilaria immitis.*

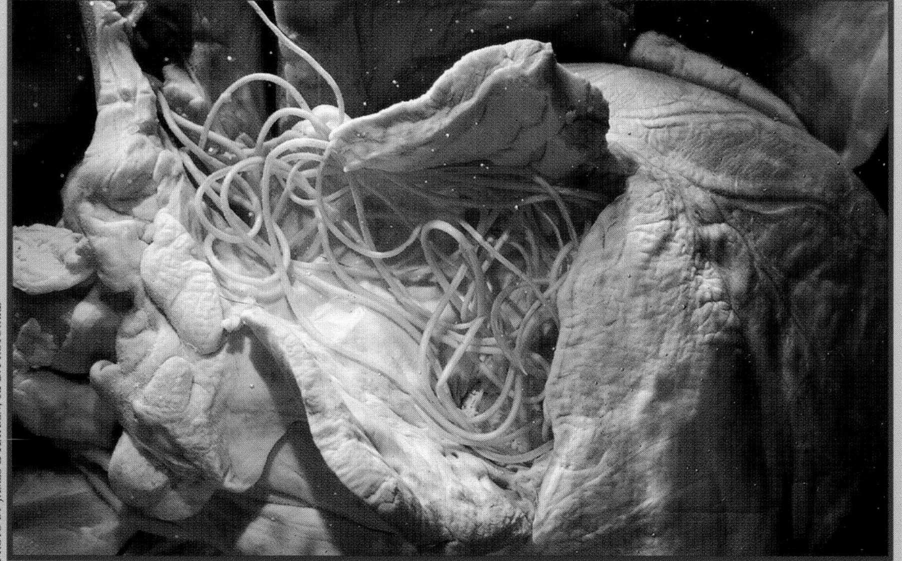
PHOTO BY JAMES E HAYDEN, RPB/PHOTOTAKE

The heart of a dog infected with canine heartworm, *Dirofilaria immitis.*

HOMEOPATHY:
an alternative to conventional medicine

'Less is Most'

Using this principle, the strength of a homeopathic remedy is measured by the number of serial dilutions that were undertaken to create it. The greater the number of serial dilutions, the greater the strength of the homeopathic remedy. The potency of a remedy that has been made by making a dilution of 1 part in 100 parts (or 1/100) is 1c or 1cH. If this remedy is subjected to a series of further dilutions, each one being 1/100, a more dilute and stronger remedy is produced. If the remedy is diluted in this way six times, it is called 6c or 6cH. A dilution of 6c is 1 part in 1000,000,000,000. In general, higher potencies in more frequent doses are better for acute symptoms and lower potencies in more infrequent doses are more useful for chronic, long-standing problems.

CURING OUR DOGS NATURALLY

Holistic medicine means treating the whole animal as a unique, perfect living being. Generally, holistic treatments do not suppress the symptoms that the body naturally produces, as do most medications prescribed by conventional doctors and vets. Holistic methods seek to cure disease by regaining balance and harmony in the patient's environment. Some of these methods include use of nutritional therapy, herbs, flower essences, aromatherapy, acupuncture, massage, chiropractic, and, of course the most popular holistic approach, homeopathy. Homeopathy is a theory or system of treating illness with small doses of substances which, if administered in larger quantities, would produce the symptoms that the patient already has. This approach is often described as 'like cures like.' Although modern veterinary medicine is geared toward the 'quick fix,' homeopathy relies on the belief that, given the time, the body is able to heal itself and return to its natural, healthy state.

Choosing a remedy to cure a problem in our dogs is the difficult part of homeopathy. Consult with your veterinary surgeon for a professional diagnosis of your dog's symptoms. Often these symptoms require immediate conventional care. If your vet is willing, and somewhat knowledgeable, you may attempt a homeopathic remedy. Be aware that cortisone prevents homeopathic remedies from working. There are hundreds of possibilities and combinations to cure many problems in dogs, from basic physical problems such as excessive moulting, fleas or other parasites, unattractive doggy odour, bad breath, upset tummy, dry, oily or dull coat, diarrhoea, ear problems or eye discharge (including tears and dry or mucousy matter), to behavioural abnormalities, such as fear of loud noises, habitual licking, poor appetite, excessive barking, obesity and various phobias. From alumina to zincum metallicum, the remedies span the planet and the imagination...from flowers and weeds to chemicals, insect droppings, diesel smoke and volcanic ash.

Using 'Like to Treat Like'

Unlike conventional medicines that suppress symptoms, homeopathic remedies treat illnesses with small doses of substances that, if administered in larger quantities, would produce the symptoms that the patient already has. Whilst the same homeopathic remedy can be used to treat different symptoms in different dogs, here are some interesting remedies and their uses.

Apis Mellifica
(made from honey bee venom) can be used for allergies or to reduce swelling that occurs in acutely infected kidneys.

Diesel Smoke
can be used to help control travel sickness.

Calcarea Fluorica
(made from calcium fluoride which helps harden bone structure) can be useful in treating hard lumps in tissues.

Natrum Muriaticum
(made from common salt, sodium chloride) is useful in treating thin, thirsty dogs.

Nitricum Acidum
(made from nitric acid) is used for symptoms you would expect to see from contact with acids such as lesions, especially where the skin joins the linings of body orifices or openings such as the lips and nostrils.

Symphytum
(made from the herb Knitbone, Symphytum officianale) is used to encourage bones to heal.

Urtica Urens
(made from the common stinging nettle) is used in treating painful, irritating rashes.

UNDERSTANDING THE BEHAVIOUR OF YOUR CHOW CHOW

As a Chow Chow owner, you have selected your dog so that you and your loved ones can have a companion, a protector, a friend and a four-legged family member. You invest time, money and effort to care for and train the family's new charge. Of course, this chosen canine behaves perfectly! Well, perfectly like a dog.

THINK LIKE A DOG

Dogs do not think like humans, nor do humans think like dogs, though we try. Unfortunately, a dog is incapable of working out how humans think, so the responsibility falls on the owner to adopt a proper canine mindset. Dogs cannot rationalise, and dogs exist in the present moment. Many dog owners make the mistake in training of thinking that they can reprimand their dog for something he did a while ago. Basically, you cannot even reprimand a dog for something he did 20 seconds ago! Either catch him in the act or forget it! It is a waste of your and your dog's time—in his mind, you are reprimanding him for whatever he is doing at that moment.

The following behavioural problems represent some which owners most commonly encounter. Every dog is unique and every situation is unique. No author could purport to solve your Chow Chow's problem simply by reading a script. Here we outline some basic 'dogspeak' so that owners' chances of solving behavioural problems are increased. Discuss bad habits with your veterinary surgeon and he/she can recommend a behavioural specialist to consult in appropriate cases. Since behavioural abnormalities are the main reason owners abandon their pets, we hope that you will make a valiant effort to solve your Chow Chow's problem. Patience and understanding are virtues that dwell in every pet-loving household.

AGGRESSION

Aggression can be a very big problem in dogs, regardless of the size or background of the breed. Aggression, when not controlled, always becomes dangerous. An aggressive dog, no matter the size, may lunge at, bite or even attack a person or another dog. Aggressive behaviour is not to be tolerated. It is painful for a family to watch their dog become unpredictable in his behaviour to the point where they are afraid of him. While not all aggressive behaviour is dangerous, growling, baring teeth, etc., can be frightening. It is important to ascertain why the dog is acting in this manner. Aggression is a display of dominance, and the dog should not have the dominant role in its pack, which is, in this case, your family.

It is important not to challenge an aggressive dog as this could provoke an attack. Observe your Chow Chow's body language. Does he make direct eye contact and stare? Does he try to make himself as large as possible: ears pricked, chest out, tail erect? Height and size signify authority in a dog pack—being taller or 'above' another dog literally means that he is 'above' in the social status. These body signals tell you that your Chow Chow thinks he is in charge, a problem that needs to be addressed. An aggressive dog is unpredictable; you never know when he is going to strike and what he is going to do. You cannot understand why a dog that is playful and loving one minute is growling and snapping the next.

The best solution is to consult a behavioural specialist, one who has experience with the Chow Chow if possible. Together, perhaps you can pinpoint the cause of your dog's aggression and do something about it. An aggressive dog cannot be trusted, and a dog that cannot be trusted is not safe to have as a family pet. If, very unusually, you find that your pet has become untrustworthy and you feel it necessary to seek a new home with a more suitable family and environment, explain fully to the new owners all your reasons for rehoming the dog to be fair to all concerned. In the very worst case, you will have to consider euthanasia.

Dogs sniff to get to know each other. It's one of the ways they assess their places in the 'pecking order' and establish who is top dog, but they should do this in a friendly manner.

Aggression toward Other Dogs

A dog's aggressive behaviour toward another dog sometimes stems from insufficient exposure to other dogs at an early age. This is yet another reason why socialisation is so vital to the Chow. If other dogs make your Chow Chow nervous and agitated, he will lash out as a defensive mechanism, though this behaviour is thankfully uncommon in the breed. A dog who has not received sufficient exposure to other canines tends to believe that he is the only dog on the planet. The animal becomes so dominant that he does not even show signs that he is fearful or threatened. Without growling or any other physical signal as a warning, he will lunge at and bite the other dog. A way to correct this is to let your Chow Chow approach another dog when walking on lead. Watch very closely and at the very first sign of aggression, correct your Chow Chow and pull him away. Scold him for any sign of discomfort, and then praise him when he ignores or tolerates the other dog. Keep this up until he stops the aggressive behaviour, learns to ignore the other dog or accepts other dogs. Praise him lavishly for his correct behaviour.

Dominant Aggression

A social hierarchy is firmly established in a wild dog pack. The dog wants to dominate those under him and please those above him. Dogs know that there must be a leader. If you are not the obvious choice for emperor, the dog will assume the throne! These conflicting innate desires are what a dog owner confronts when he sets about training a dog. In training a dog to obey commands, the owner is reinforcing that he is the top dog in the 'pack' and that the dog should, and should want to, serve his superior. Thus, the owner is suppressing the dog's urge to dominate by modifying his behaviour and making him obedient.

An important part of training is taking every opportunity to reinforce that you are the leader. The simple action of making your Chow Chow sit to wait for his food says that you control when he eats and that he is dependent on you for food. Although it may be difficult, do not give in to your dog's wishes every time he whines at you or looks at you with his pleading eyes. It is a constant effort to show the dog that his place in the pack is at the bottom. This is not meant to sound cruel or inhumane. You love your Chow Chow and you should treat him with care and affection. You (hopefully) did not get a dog just so you could control another creature. Dog training is not about being cruel or feeling important, it is about moulding the dog's behaviour into what is acceptable and teaching him to live by your rules. In theory, it is quite simple: catch him in appropriate behaviour and reward him for it. Add a dog into the equation and it becomes a bit more trying, but as a rule of thumb, positive reinforcement is what works best.

With a dominant dog, punishment and negative reinforcement can have the opposite effect of what you are after. It can make a dog fearful and/or act out aggressively if he feels he is being challenged. Remember, a dominant dog perceives himself at the top of the social heap and will fight to defend his perceived status. The best way to prevent that is never to give him reason to think that he is in control in the first place. If you are having trouble training your Chow Chow and it seems as if he is constantly challenging your authority, seek the help of an obedience trainer or behavioural specialist. A professional will work with both you and your dog to teach you effective techniques to use at home. Beware of trainers who rely on excessively harsh methods; scolding is necessary now and then, but the focus in your training should always be on positive reinforcement.

If you can isolate what brings out the fear reaction, you can help the dog overcome it. Supervise your Chow Chow's interactions with people and other dogs, and praise the dog when it goes well. If he starts to act aggressively in a situation, correct him and remove him from the situation. Do not let people approach the dog and start petting him without your express permission. That way, you can have the dog sit to accept petting, and praise him when he behaves properly. You are focusing on praise and on modifying his behaviour by rewarding him when he acts appropriately. By being gentle and by supervising his interactions, you are showing him that there is no need to be afraid or defensive.

SEXUAL BEHAVIOUR

Dogs exhibit certain sexual behaviours that may have influenced your choice of male or female when you first purchased your Chow Chow. To a certain extent, spaying/neutering will eliminate these behaviours, but if you are purchasing a dog that you wish to breed from, you should be aware of what you will have to deal with throughout the dog's life.

Female dogs usually have two oestruses per year with each season lasting about three weeks. These are the only times in which a female dog will mate, and she usually will not allow this until the second week of the cycle, but this does vary from bitch to bitch. If not bred during the heat cycle, a bitch may experience a false pregnancy, in which her mammary glands swell and she exhibits maternal tendencies toward toys or other objects.

Owners must further recognise that mounting is not merely a sexual expression but also one of dominance. Be consistent and persistent and you will find that you can 'move mounters.'

SMILE!

Dogs and humans may be the only animals that smile. Dogs imitate the smile on their owner's face when he greets a friend. The dog only smiles at

its human friends. It never smiles at another dog or cat. Usually it rolls up its lips and shows its teeth in a clenched mouth while it rolls over onto its back begging for a soft scratch.

CHEWING

The national canine pastime is chewing! Every dog loves to sink his 'canines' into a tasty bone, but sometimes that bone is in his owner's hand! Dogs need to chew, to massage their gums, to make their new teeth feel better and to exercise their jaws. This is a natural behaviour deeply embedded in all things canine. Our role as owners is not to stop the dog's chewing, but to redirect it to positive, chew-worthy objects. Be an informed owner and purchase proper chew toys like strong nylon bones that will not splinter. Be sure that the objects are safe and durable, since your dog's safety is at risk. Again, the owner is responsible for ensuring a dog-proof environment. The best answer is prevention; that is, put your shoes, handbags and other tasty objects in their proper places (out of the reach of the growing canine mouth). Direct puppies to their toys whenever you see them tasting the furniture legs or the leg of your trousers. Make a loud noise to attract the pup's attention and immediately escort him to his chew toy and engage him with the toy for at least four minutes, praising and encouraging him all the while.

Some trainers recommend deterrents, such as hot pepper, a bitter spice or a product designed for this purpose, to discourage the dog from chewing unwanted objects. Test these products yourself before investing in a large quantity.

JUMPING UP

Jumping up is a dog's friendly way of saying hello! Some dog owners do not mind when their dog jumps up. The problem arises when guests come to the house and the dog greets them in the same manner—whether they like it or not! However friendly the greeting may be, the chances are that your visitors will not appreciate your dog's enthusiasm.

The dog will not be able to distinguish upon whom he can jump and whom he cannot. Therefore, it is probably best to discourage this behaviour entirely.

Pick a command such as 'Off.' (avoid using 'Down' since you will use that for the dog to lie down) and tell him 'Off' when he jumps up. Place him on the ground on all fours and have him sit, praising him the whole time. Always lavish him with praise and petting when he is in the sit position. In this way you can give him a warm affectionate greeting, let him know that you are as excited to see him as he is to see you and instil good manners at the same time!

DIGGING

Digging, which is seen as a destructive behaviour to humans, is actually quite a natural behaviour in dogs. Although terriers (the 'earth dogs') are most associated with the digging, any dog's desire to dig can be irrepressible and most frustrating to his owners. When digging occurs in your garden, it is actually a normal behaviour redirected into something the dog can do in his everyday life. In the wild, a dog would be actively seeking food, making his own shelter, etc. He would be using his paws in a purposeful manner for his survival. Since you provide him with food and shelter, he has no need to use his paws for these purposes, and so the energy that he would be using may manifest itself in the form of little holes all over your garden and flower beds.

Perhaps your dog is digging as a reaction to boredom—it is somewhat similar to someone eating a whole bag of crisps in front of the TV—because they are there and there is nothing better to do! Basically, the answer is to provide the dog with adequate play and exercise so that his mind and paws are occupied, and so that he feels as if he is doing something useful.

Of course, digging is easiest to control if it is stopped as soon as

Think twice before encouraging your Chow to jump up. You may not mind if it becomes a habit, but guests to your home may not appreciate your dog greeting them this way.

The nose knows! Dogs that are bored will dig...especially once they've found a particularly pleasing place. Discourage your Chow from this behaviour immediately.

possible, but it is often hard to catch a dog in the act. If your dog is a compulsive digger and is not easily distracted by other activities, you can designate an area on your property where he is allowed to dig. If you catch him digging in an off-limits area of the garden, immediately bring him to the approved area and praise him for digging there. Keep a close eye on him so that you can catch him in the act—that is the only way to make him understand what is permitted and what is not. If you take him to a hole he dug an hour ago and tell him 'No,' he will understand that you are not fond of holes, or dirt, or flowers. If you catch him while he is stifle-deep in your tulips, that is when he will get your message.

BARKING

Dogs cannot talk—oh, what they would say if they could! Instead, barking is a dog's way of 'talking.' It can be somewhat frustrating because it is not always easy to tell what a dog means by his bark—is he excited, happy, frightened or angry? Whatever it is that the dog is trying to say, he should not be punished for barking. It is only when the barking becomes excessive, and when the excessive barking becomes a bad habit, that the behaviour needs to be modified. Fortunately, Chow Chows are not as vocal as most other dogs, and they tend to use their barks more purposefully. If an intruder came into your home in the middle of the night and your Chow Chow barked a warning, wouldn't you be pleased? You would probably deem your dog a hero, a wonderful guardian and protector of the home. Most dogs are not as discriminating as the Chow Chow. For instance, if a friend drops by unexpectedly and rings the doorbell and is greeted with a sudden sharp bark, you would probably be annoyed with the dog. In reality, isn't this just the same behaviour? The dog does not know any better. Unless he sees who is at the door and it is someone he knows, he will bark as a means of vocalising that his (and your) territory is being threatened. Barking is his means of letting you know that there is an intrusion, whether friend or foe, on your property. This type of barking is instinctive and should not be discouraged.

Excessive habitual barking, however, is a problem that should be corrected early on. As your Chow Chow grows up, you will be able to tell when his barking is purposeful and when it is for no reason. You will become able to distinguish your dog's different barks and their meanings. For example, the bark when someone comes to the door will be different from the bark when he is excited to see you. It is similar to a person's tone of voice, except that the dog has to rely totally on tone of voice because he does not have the benefit of using words. An incessant barker will be evident at an early age.

There are some things that encourage a dog to bark. For example, if your dog barks non-stop for a few minutes and you give him a treat to quieten him, he believes that you are rewarding him for barking. He will associate barking with getting a treat, and will keep doing it until he is rewarded.

FOOD STEALING

Is your dog devising ways of stealing food from your coffee table? If so, you must answer the following questions: Is your Chow Chow hungry, or is he 'constantly famished' like many dogs seem to be? Face it, some dogs are more food-motivated than others. They are totally obsessed by the smell of food and can only think of their next meal. Food stealing is terrific fun and always yields a great result—FOOD, glorious food.

The owner's goal, therefore, is to be sensible about where food is placed in the home, and to reprimand your dog whenever he is caught in the act of stealing. But remember, only reprimand your dog if you actually see him stealing, not later when the crime is discovered for that will be of no use at all and will only serve to confuse.

DID YOU KNOW?

The number of dogs who suffer from separation anxiety is on the rise as more and more pet owners find themselves at work all day. New

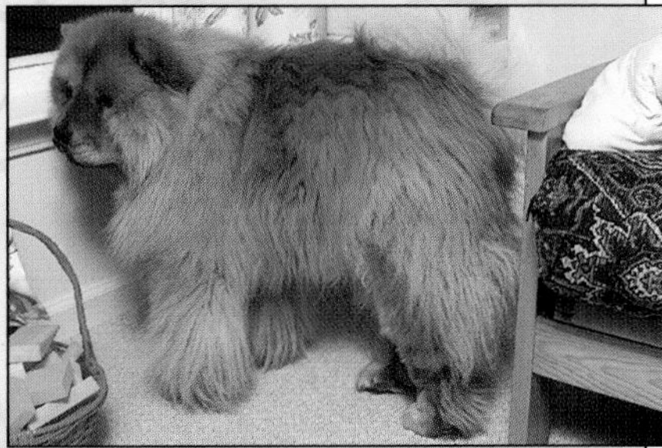

attention is being paid to this problem, which is especially hard to diagnose since it is only evident when the dog is alone. Research is currently being done to help educate dog owners about separation anxiety and how they can help minimise this problem in their dogs.

BEGGING

Just like food stealing, begging is a favourite pastime of hungry puppies! It achieves that same lovely objective—FOOD! Dogs quickly learn that their owners keep the 'good food' for themselves, and that we humans do not dine on dried food alone. Begging is a conditioned response related to a specific stimulus, time and place. The sounds of the kitchen, cans and bottles opening, crinkling bags, the smell of food in preparation, etc., will excite the dog and soon the paws are in the air!

Here is the solution to stopping this behaviour: Never give in to a beggar! You are rewarding the dog for sitting pretty, jumping up, whining and rubbing his nose into you by giving him what he's after—food. By ignoring the dog, you will (eventually) force the behaviour into extinction. Note that the behaviour is likely to get worse before it disappears, so be sure there are not any 'softies' in the family who will give in to little 'Oliver' every time he whimpers, 'More, please.'

SEPARATION ANXIETY

Your Chow Chow may howl, whine or otherwise vocalise his displeasure at your leaving the house and his being left alone. This is a normal reaction, no different from the child who cries as his mother leaves him on the first day at school. In fact, constant attention can lead to separation anxiety in the first place. If you are endlessly fussing over your dog, he will come to expect this from you all of the time and it will be more traumatic for him when you are not there. Obviously, you enjoy spending time with your dog, and he thrives on your love and attention. However, it should not become a dependent relationship where he is heartbroken without you.

One thing you can do to minimise separation anxiety is to make your entrances and exits as low-key as possible. Do not give your dog a long drawn-out goodbye, and do not overly lavish him with hugs and kisses when you return. This is giving in to the attention that he craves, and it will only make him miss it more when you are away. Another thing you can try is to give your dog a treat when you leave; this will not only keep him occupied and keep his mind off the fact that you have just left, but it will also help him associate your leaving with a pleasant experience.

You may have to accustom your dog to being left alone at intervals. Of course, when your dog starts whimpering as you approach the door, your first instinct will be to run to him and comfort him, but do not do it! Really—eventually he will adjust to your absence. His anxiety stems from being placed in an unfamiliar situation; by familiarising him with being alone he will learn that he will survive. That is not to say you should purposely leave your dog home alone, but the dog needs to know that while he can depend on you for his care, you do not have to be by his side 24 hours a day.

When the dog is alone in the house, he should be confined to his designated dog-proof area of the house. This should be the area in which he sleeps and already feels comfortable so he will feel more at ease when he is alone.

COPROPHAGIA

Faeces eating is, to most humans, one of the most disgusting behaviours that their dog could engage in, yet to the dog it is perfectly normal. It is hard for us to understand why a dog would want to eat its own faeces. He could be seeking certain nutrients that are missing from his diet; he could be just plain hungry; or he could be attracted by the pleasing (to a dog) scent. While coprophagia most often refers to the dog eating his own faeces, a dog may just as likely eat that of another animal as well if he comes across it. Vets have found that diets with a low digestibility, containing relatively low levels of fibre and high levels of starch, increase coprophagia. Therefore, high-fibre diets may decrease the likelihood of dogs eating faeces. Both the consistency of the stool (how firm it feels in the dog's mouth) and the presence of undigested nutrients increase the likelihood. Dogs often find the stool of cats and horses more palatable than that of other dogs. Once the dog develops diarrhoea from faeces eating, it will likely stop this distasteful habit.

To discourage this behaviour, first make sure that the food you are feeding your dog is nutritionally complete and that he is getting enough food. If changes in his diet do not seem to work, and no medical cause can be found, you will have to modify the behaviour through environmental control before it becomes a habit. The best way to prevent your dog from eating his stool is to make it unavailable—clean up after he eliminates and remove any stool from the garden. If it is not there, he cannot eat it.

Reprimanding for stool eating rarely impresses the dog. Vets recommend distracting the dog while he is in the act of stool eating. Coprophagia is seen most frequently in pups 6 to 12 months of age, and usually disappears around the dog's first birthday.

INDEX

*Page numbers in **boldface** indicate illustrations.*

My Chow Chow

PUT YOUR PUPPY'S FIRST PICTURE HERE

Dog's Name ______________________________

Date ______________ Photographer ______________________